Debugging the Mind

THE

Path to a
Balanced Life

SIVA MANGALAM

Debugging THE Mind

Path to a Balanced Life

SIVA MANGALAM

ISBN: 978-1-7355811-0-1 (paperback)
ISBN: 978-1-7355811-1-8 (e-book)

Printed in the United States of America.

Cover Design by 100Covers.com
Interior Design by FormattedBooks.com
Edited by Bookhelpline.com

CONTENTS

INTRODUCTION

*Seeking a Messiah for liberation is like a fish
searching for an Olympics swim coach.*

We are the only ones with access to our minds. No one can violate, steal, alter, or corrupt our minds without our cooperation. Two millennia ago, Marcus Aurelius observed (Piazza 2008): "You have control over your mind but not over external events. Realize it and be free." When Zen Master Linji said (Kopp 1976), "If you meet a Buddha on the road, kill him," he was not inciting homicide, but merely wished to convey that nirvana cannot be outsourced.

What Marcus Aurelius and Linji conveyed may be self-evident, but it is difficult to comprehend why fear, anxiety, deception, substance abuse, addiction, depression, suicide, homicide, and violence are widespread even among the affluent in *free societies*.

According to the World Health Organization (WHO), there is a suicide every 40 seconds and over 300 million people suffer from anxiety disorders (WHO 2017). Death by suicide is second only to death in road accidents among the young. Nearly 40 million people or one-in-five adults in the USA suffer from anxiety that is rampaging through society like a pandemic (NIMH 2017). The spread of Covid-19 (Ahorsu, et al. 2020) seems to have made the situation worse.

For most people, the situation may not be as morbid as these statistics might suggest, but it is not a bed of roses either. It is usually a life filled with pesky nuisance.

It reminds me of my childhood in India when I had to walk or run barefoot on a rough path to the railway station to catch the morning train to school. My soles bled when I inadvertently stepped on sticky thorns or needle-sharp pebbles. It was painful as the soles are especially tender early in the morning. My mind eventually developed a spatial layout of the areas that were laden with sharp pebbles and thorns, and I became adept at avoiding them even in the dark!

Our life resembles a similar obstacle course to reach a desired destination. We try to avoid sharp pebbles and prickly thorns that have taken the avatar of pesky human beings. However, unlike the passive and stationary pebbles and thorns, troublesome human beings are aggressive, shift their positions, and push the invisible buttons that trigger emotions within us.

I encountered such people in my life. I was leading a charmed life, conducting exciting research at NASA when a series of jolts caught me off guard and threw me off balance.* I was deceived, vilified, threatened, and thrown under the bus by those I looked up to, respected, and trusted; by those who had helped me in the past; and by those whom I had helped. I was rebuffed when I tried to find equitable solutions. I could have clammed up to avoid getting hurt, but it would have simultaneously blocked the door to creative expression. The challenge was to keep the door open but not get hurt, which is the goal of *Debugging the Mind.*

The fundamental question I address is: given the fact that we have control over our minds, how do we let others disturb our minds? How do mere spoken, or written words, and denial of friendship, and opportunities have a strong impact on our emotions? What within us is getting pricked and hurt? Is our mind infested with *bugs?* If it is, how do we *debug the mind?*

The Challenge

Bugs that cause physical illness and pain have physical existence (e.g., microorganisms), but bugs that trigger mental disturbances are abstract. They are invisible to sensory organs and scientific tools. They may not even be alive, but their mere appearance in the form of words, books, pictures, statues, or symbols trigger strong emotions. If the bugs are allowed to fester, they may spread, grow with time, and make people belligerent. Development of an effective path to

---

* Described in Chapter 2 on **Journey in Search of My Self.**

eradicate abstract bugs and restore mental balance is, perhaps, the greatest challenge facing us.

Philosophy, psychology, neuroscience, religion, and spirituality are concerned with the mind.

Philosophy is speculative. Psychology deals with problems that vary from person to person. As race, religion, culture, gender, social status, and upbringing play a critical role in the psychological makeup of a person, psychology does not offer a uniformly valid solution that is applicable to all people. Neuroscience is making rapid strides, but it is still grappling with the mysterious nature of emotions (Adolphs 2018).

Religions try to placate mythical beings with superstitious rituals and prayers for liberation from the metaphysical bugs. Religious followers today are no closer to liberation than their predecessors were two millennia ago. Instead of eradicating the bug, they have infected the world with various mutations of the metaphysical bug.

Zen, Yoga, Transcendental Meditation, mindfulness meditation, etc. are popular spiritual practices to calm the mind. They result in a mind that behaves like an efficient air-conditioner with small fluctuations about a desired mean value, but the continuous chatter can be quite annoying and hard to eliminate.

Debugging the Mind

In stark contrast, *Debugging the Mind* presents a radically different approach to completely obliterate the metaphysical bug, once and for all. Instead of blindly searching for the invisible metaphysical bug or vainly hoping for mythical beings to protect us, *Debugging the Mind* starts with a known solution and systematically eliminates the known barriers to its realization.

Debugging the Mind is based on two principles that are innately known to every individual:

1. *Do not do to others what you would not want them to do to you* (the first principle).
2. *Maintain feelings, thoughts, words, and actions in harmony* (the second principle).

The first principle is the necessary condition that must be fulfilled for the realization of mental balance. The second principle is the sufficiency condition for mental balance.

As internal discord among *feelings, thoughts, words, and actions* is the known cause of mental disturbances, mental wellbeing is realized when the known internal discord is eliminated. *Debugging the Mind* is based on facts and not fiction. It is self-consistent and self-sufficient. It is independent of external authority. Mental balance is directly realized through exploration and experimentation, and not through speculation, and logical argumentation.

Debugging the Mind is a pragmatic three-phase approach that consists of **prevention**, **exploration**, and **experimentation.**

Prevention is based on the first principle, "*do not do to others what you would not want them to do to you.*" It is the well-known Hillel-Kongzi Golden Rule (Allinson 2003); a basic precept in all religions. The first principle is not a moral injunction but a prophylactic measure to prevent bugs (mental disturbances) from taking root in the mind. When practiced, it creates a calm mind and a kindred spirit. As the perceived need to judge, condemn, and seek revenge vanishes, it opens up enormous mental space for creativity.

Consuming poison has an almost immediate effect on our physical health. Ill-effects of drinking polluted water may take a little longer to manifest. The harmful effects of unhygienic practices may take even longer to manifest in a perceptible manner. In sharp contrast, one may never recognize a direct correlation between the violation of the first principle and its adverse effects on our mental wellbeing. We do not have scientific proof for it. It is a heuristic.

It is worth noting that even without access to modern scientific tools like microscopes to recognize the existence of microorganisms, some ancient cultures intuitively or through empirical evidence realized the need for hygiene. Similarly, they also seem to have realized the need for practicing the first principle for mental wellbeing.

The first principle, "*Do not do to others what you would not want them to do to you*" is simple to state but hard to implement when we are exposed to anger, hatred, jealousy, contempt, deception, and various kinds of mental and physical abuse from other people. We also encounter people who badmouth us, cut us off on the highway, jump the queue, belittle us, berate us, and threaten us in many ways in our daily life. We have little control over them. When we are gentle, helpful, and harmless, others may mistake us for being weak and meek. On the other hand, responding in kind is likely to be escalated and followed by endless conflicts. Human history is replete with this madness. We can see it repeated every day, locally, and globally.

How to maintain mental balance and robust mental health in such an environment is a challenge that all of us face. *Debugging the Mind* meets this challenge with **Exploration** *of the mind* in Phase II and **Experimentation** *with the mind* in Phase III.

Exploration of the nature of the mental disturbances that have already taken root in the mind is the equivalent of diagnosis of physical illness in medicine. Meditative practices of Patanjali's *Ashtanga Yoga Sutra* (eight-fold yoga) (Ranganathan 2014) are used as a diagnostic technique to explore the mind. *Debugging the Mind* provides a rational explanation of how the diligent practice of the eight-fold yoga will not only calm the mind but will also reveal our weaknesses that cause *discord among feelings, thoughts, words, and actions.*

Systematic **experimentation** in Phase III is based on the understanding that discord among *feelings, thoughts, words, and actions* arises from relative weaknesses in our cognitive functions (*thinking, feeling, and sensing*) that are used to perceive and respond to reality (Berens 1999). When some of them are weak in relation to others, they cause emotional imbalance and mental disturbances. Harmony is achieved when we realize innate balance among them.

Historically, people with physical strength (*sensing*) and intellectual power (*thinking*) have dominated the world, and others have tried to emulate them. A tripod with two relatively long legs (*sensing* and *thinking*) and a stunted third leg (*feeling*) is naturally unbalanced regardless of how strong the long legs are. A metaphorical fall followed by mental suffering is inevitable for anyone with such an unbalanced mind. Only feelings of love, camaraderie, and compassion can restore balance and make the mind robust. I believe that those who are innately strong in *feelings* and *intuition*, especially women, will play a vital role in spreading balanced and joyful life in the next phase of human evolution. There is a lot for both men and women to learn from each other and become equal partners to realize that potential.

I am not a religious person, but I have not thrown out the baby with the bathwater.

A rational explanation of how the teachings of the Buddha (Kornfield 2012), Jesus (Stein 1994), and Muhammad (Armstrong 1992) help realize mental balance or harmony (nirvana, liberation, or inner peace) is presented without invoking esoteric doctrines, mythical beings, superstitious rituals, man-made morals, or external authority.

Debugging the Mind does not require religious scholarship, philosophical erudition, or scientific expertise; childlike curiosity to explore one's own mind through diligent practice and an innate urge to realize mental harmony will suffice. Healthy skepticism with an open mind and a keen sense of humor to laugh at oneself will help make rapid progress.

Debugging the Mind is like the training wheels used by children to learn to ride a bicycle without knowing Newtonian mechanics, biomechanics, or bicycle dynamics. Once physical balance is intuitively realized, the skill to ride a bicycle without a physical fall stays with them for life. Similarly, once mental balance is intuitively realized, the ability to lead a fearless and fulfilling life without a metaphorical fall becomes second nature.

Debugging the Mind will help parents and teachers raise emotionally well-balanced and healthy children. *Debugging the Mind* will benefit the younger generations to break free from the divisive, biased, and misogynistic traditional approaches, and lead fearless, playful, and creative lives with camaraderie and cooperation. Both religious and non-religious people can benefit from *Debugging the Mind* and bring peace to themselves and the rest of humanity.

A world humming with authentic, free, fearless, playful, creative, and enthusiastic people is not a utopian ideal, but real. It will happen one individual at a time. When people realize how absurdly simple *Debugging the Mind* is, freedom will spread faster than any known pandemic, because it is our innate nature. Thucydides observed over two millennia ago (Zagorin 2005), "Happiness comes from freedom and freedom comes from courage." We need courage to follow our innate nature. How complicated can that be!

Abraham, the Buddha, Jesus, Krishna, Laozi, Mahavir, Muhammad, Nanak, Patanjali, Socrates, Vedic Rishis, Zarathustra, and others sprinkled beautiful flowers in the form of precepts, teachings, parables, and insights to guide people. I have used my understanding to string together a garland of these flowers and present it you as *Debugging the Mind.*

Book Outline

Debugging the Mind is described in two parts.

Part I is devoted to the **Nature of the Mind** as we perceive it.

Chapter 1 describes my **Fictional Conversations with Ancient Iconoclasts** to elucidate their insights without invoking esoteric doctrines, mythical beings, superstitious rituals, man-made morals, and external authority.

Chapter 2 describes **My Journey in Search of My Self**, what prompted it, and how I lost everything (my self-image) to gain everything (my freedom).

Chapter 3 describes **The Four Paths** to liberation based on the four cognitive functions: *sensing, feeling, thinking,* and *intuition*.

Chapter 4 is on **The Language of Nature** and how science and religion describe nature in almost identical language. How dualistic human language has obfuscated our understanding of the true nature of reality and resulted in human suffering is explained.

Part II is devoted to **Debugging the Mind**.

Chapter 5 briefly describes **The Three-phase Approach** based on two fundamental principles.

Chapter 6 is on the **Prevention** of mental disturbances (bugs) from taking root in the mind. It explains the significance of the first principle and how the Ten Commandments or the *yama* and *niyama* of Yoga fulfill it.

Chapter 7 on **Exploration** provides a rational explanation of the eight-fold *Yoga Sutra* for conducting self-inquiry and how it could lead to intuitive realization of mental balance.

Chapter 8 on **Experimentation** describes practices to realize *harmony among feelings, thoughts, words and actions*. This chapter includes an unconventional look at the lives and teachings of the Buddha, Jesus, and Muhammad without introducing mythical beings and miracles.

PART I

Nature of the Mind

PROLOGUE

I had little knowledge or interest in religion, philosophy, psychology, spirituality, and neuroscience when I began the journey* to debug my mind. It turned out to be most fortuitous because ignorance can do wonders when we are aware of it and are willing to learn. I had greatly benefited from my ignorance, even while doing technical research at NASA.

I was conducting wind-tunnel tests on a family of high-performance airfoils that I had designed under the guidance of my mentor, Dr. Pfenninger, a brilliant aeronautical engineer. A friendly electronic technician came to me waving a thin, flexible sheet of sensors and asked me whether I would be interested in using them in my research. I had never before seen or used those sensors, but as I was excited to learn, I did not wait for a second invitation. It took a couple of days to meticulously instrument one of my airfoils with his sensors and begin testing.

The electronic screen showed several rows of signals from sensors that were located at different points on the airfoil. They resembled wiggly lines from an electrocardiogram. He pointed at signals from a sensor that were far more chaotic than signals from sensors that were located upstream of it and told me that the flow had separated from the airfoil at that location. I found out later that his conclusion was in accord with prevailing scientific literature.

Had I been *knowledgeable* about the sensor technology at the time of the experiment, I might have agreed with him and none would have been the wiser. But I was ignorant.

On the other hand, as the designer of the airfoil, I knew approximately where the flow separated from the airfoil. I had also conducted tests with a

---

* Described in Chapter 2 on **Journey in Search of My Self**.

modified stethoscope to identify the flow separation location by comparing the noise levels at different points on the airfoil. It was dead silence where the flow separated from the airfoil and very noisy downstream of it. It also indicated a local minimum in noise level at the flow separation location, which was quite close to the point indicated by the technician, but only slightly upstream. Initially, I thought that the small difference could be due to instrument error, but the stethoscope results gave me a hunch that his sensors may also exhibit a significant drop in magnitude in the vicinity of the separation location.

I asked the technician if he could obtain the magnitude of low-frequency signals from sensors located near the point where I thought flow separation occurred. He could and he did. Lo and behold! As expected, signal magnitude dramatically dropped at that location. In addition, low-frequency fluctuations revealed a *phase-reversal signature* across the separation point, a phenomenon that was previously unknown. It was my "Eureka" moment. My intuition based on flow physics coupled with his impeccable expertise in electronics led to the discovery.

We received several NASA awards and patents for the discovery that is of considerable value for flow control applications in aeronautical, marine, and wind engineering.

I was in a similar situation with regard to my emotional trauma with a major difference: my mental disturbances were inaccessible to scientific tools. I only knew that I was hurt, but clueless about what exactly was hurt and totally ignorant about how to overcome it. I was certain that I did not intentionally hurt anyone. If anything, I had helped. My attempts to resolve the problems were of no avail. I was rebuffed. Some of them apologized to me years later. One of them took twenty years to do so, when he was terminally ill. As they were uncooperative, and I had no access to their minds, I decided to explore my own mind to which I had direct access.

I sought solitude. I spent over four months in a Japanese Zen monastery, where I did *zazen* (a sitting meditation) for an average of over eight hours a day. It was an ideal setting for me—quiet, well-organized, disciplined, and supportive. No newspapers, no TV, no telephone, no computer, no books, and no gossip. My stay at the monastery calmed my mind.

Then, out of the blue, I realized the phantom nature of the problem and burst out laughing. By saying this, I am not trivializing the seriousness of the problem that had made me cry so many nights. I was laughing at the paradoxical nature of what I found (or did not find): *I went in search of my self but found no-self.* Discord among feelings, thoughts, words, and actions naturally vanish when there is no-self.

It was amusing to realize that self-image was like the shadow of a body cast by light or its reflection in a mirror. Self-image is merely a projection of our mind that is cast by others. We can learn a lot about ourselves from how our so-called enemies respond to us. Thus, it makes sense to love our enemies as they are our best teachers!

This unexpected realization made me curious to know how religions addressed the problem. What I found blew my mind away, as I tended to look at all religions as hocus-pocus.

I was astonished to realize that Abraham, the Buddha, Jesus, Krishna, Laozi, Mahavir, Muhammad, Nanak, Patanjali, and Zarathustra knew how to *debug the mind.* Being an atheist, I was pleasantly surprised to find that every one of them, without an exception, rejected all prevailing religions and gods. They were iconoclasts to their contemporaries.

As their insights were not intellectual but were based on emotions that transcend reason, *Debugging the Mind* begins with a chapter on my fictitious conversations with them to intuitively grasp their insights. It is an attempt to circumvent logical and linguistic obfuscations introduced by traditional religious interpretations with dualistic values.

I take on the dual role of a skeptical religious person and an open-minded non-religious person asking them to elucidate their insights. In actuality, it is a conversation with oneself, where we can be totally blunt and quickly get to the bottom line. The questions and answers given in this fictitious encounter are those that were relevant to me when I was still searching for an answer. They are included here primarily as a template for readers who are interested in having similar conversations in privacy, as perceptions of reality and life experience vary from person to person. The true meaning and purpose of their insights are left to the intuitive understanding of the reader.

Conversations with Ancient Iconoclasts

Nobody errs knowingly and willingly.
—**Socrates** *(Segvic 2000)*

I t is amazing how everything in the universe, from tiny sub-atomic particles to huge galaxies, and from microscopic organisms to large mammals, seems to know its precise role in the cosmic drama. In stark contrast, my mind is vainly and restlessly worried about its future in the *"to be or not to be"*—mode, with fear, anxiety, and uncertainty. I have often wondered what it would take to spontaneously live in the present and peacefully enjoy the free ride in choiceless awareness.

What did the great iconoclasts of the ancient past know that I don't? What made the Buddha (Kornfield 2012) abandon the comforts of a princely life and lead the spartan life of a mendicant for over four decades? How did the gentle Jesus (Stein 1994) face crucifixion with forgiveness and grace without any trace of animosity toward the perpetrators of the heinous act? What prompted Krishna (Fosse 2007) to transfer his hundred-thousand strong army to fight on behalf of the enemy and be an unarmed charioteer in a war that saw the slaughter of hundreds of thousands of warriors? What moved Mahavir (Paniker 2010) to cease harming all life, including insects? What made Muhammad (Armstrong 1992) bear relentless persecution and threat of death from the rulers of Mecca and yet preach peace, emancipate women, free slaves, and practice universal camaraderie? How did Socrates (Church 1887) drink hemlock with fortitude, forbearance, and without fear or sorrow? What made these remarkable men so compassionate even at the doors of death and destruction that make me tremble with fear and anxiety?

It is amply clear that material gains, fame, social status, political power, legacy, or a place in history were of little interest to them. They were not concerned even about their own survival. If anything, they seem to have gone freely and fearlessly in the very opposite direction.

It is possible to dismiss them as deluded, impractical, and unreal (not historical) people. Or, suggest that they were specially chosen by God. However, even if they were a figment of my imagination, their ingenious insights resonate within me in an inexplicable manner and, like haunting melodies that simultaneously evoke sadness and tears of joy, they elevate my emotions to a different level for no apparent reason, reminding me of the memorable line from Keats: "Heard melodies are sweet, but those unheard are sweeter" (Keats 1997).

They knew something precious that has remained elusive and mysterious. I was eager to know what it was. Was it accessible to me? If yes, how do I find it? What makes me desperately cling to the fleeting life that they so readily gave up? What would it take for me to be convinced that whatever they did would also be right and natural for me to do if I were to face a similar predicament in my life? Is it possible to practice their teachings and lead a normal life in society?

Ironically, *every religious founder, from Abraham to Zarathustra, rejected all the prevailing religions and their gods and pressed the reset button.* I wanted to know what they rejected and what they asserted instead. I could not understand how there could be so many religions with so many gods. All of them cannot simultaneously be right. As I was going through these thoughts on a cool autumn day under a clear blue sky, a *miracle* occurred.*

I was approaching the end of my habitual reverie in the quiet wooded environs of the house, when loud music and revelry broke the eerie silence. I suddenly found myself amidst a lively crowd. I was amazed to realize that the revelers included Abraham, the Buddha, Hillel, Jesus, Kongzi, Krishna, Laozi, Mahavir, Moses, Muhammad, Nanak, Patanjali, Socrates, Vedic Rishis,

---

* I have assumed poetic freedom to let the ancients speak for themselves. I have also done so in some later chapters for more effective communication. I have friendly and frank conversations with them, just like I do with loved ones. No disrespect is intended to anyone. Of course, there was no hallucination or miracle!

Zarathustra, and Zhuangzi! They were so unlike the somber folks portrayed in literature.

Bursting out with laughter at my bewilderment, Zarathustra teased, "If you have the right spirit (*no pun intended*) life is a celebration!"

Jesus kept the party in stitches, sprinkling in a few juicy jokes that he had borrowed from Osho to add spice to his sermons. Socrates apparently had not given up on corrupting the Athenian youth with the truth. Abraham was trying to make it up with Muhammad for having abandoned Hagar and Ishmael in the Arabian desert. He insisted that oil was fair compensation, but Muhammad was not buying the argument. Zarathustra was laughing at their discomfiture. Hillel was standing on one leg reciting the Torah. Patanjali was practicing yoga, the Hindu sages were chanting the Vedas, Krishna was dancing with *Gopikas*, Laozi and Zhuangzi were exchanging rib-tickling jokes on Kongzi, and the Buddha was doing *zazen* amidst all the tumult.

I was ecstatic when they volunteered to elucidate the meaning and purpose of their precepts and teachings. It was beyond my wildest dreams to hear them share their insights on how indiscriminate application of logic led me into a rabbit hole with false perceptions of reality, and how the practice of their precepts and teachings would expose my ignorance and reveal the truth that liberates. At school, I was used to seeing one teacher standing in front of a classroom full of students. Here, I was a single student standing in front of top-notch masters. It was surreal.

Muhammad

At the very outset, all of them, and Muhammad in particular, emphatically rejected god(s), image worship, supercilious rituals, and superstitions. With twinkling eyes, Muhammad said that he asked his disciples to recite, *"La Ilaha Il' Allah"* (There is no God, only Allah), five times a day to make it abundantly clear that there is no God, only Allah.

I asked, "If there is no God, who is Allah?"

"Allah is Allah," he said cryptically, which sounded more like, Allah is a law.

I persisted, "Why did you deny God instead of simply asserting the existence of Allah?"

"God is a fictitious invention of fearful primitive people. Allah is not a fiction. Allah is real. Realization of Allah would make you playful, merciful, compassionate, and creative. In stark contrast, the fictitious image of God, along with his alter-ego Satan make you fearful, weak, ignorant, jealous, avaricious, superstitious, and servile."

"Is that why you rejected image worship?"

"Yes, of course. By definition, images are unreal. A photograph is only an image and not the real object. Even the image of God that you worship is in your head. When you worship, one part of your brain is worshiping an image in another part of your own brain. In other words, worship of any kind, with or without idols, is self-worshiping and narcissistic."

"Allah needs no worship," Muhammad continued. "Allah cannot be placated with platitudes and flattery. Allah treats everyone alike. It is a healthy attitude to be thankful (*shukriya*) for the generosity and compassion of Allah. However, mere intellectual speculation is useless if you are not aware of Allah. Logic and reason would only lead to relative truths but cannot reveal the absolute truth. You must focus efforts on directly knowing Allah. Do that and be free of fear and anxiety. You will fall in love with Allah and surrender, as peace descends on you. Life becomes blissful. I called it Islam."

"If not God, what is Allah," I stubbornly insisted.

Muhammad patiently answered, "Allah is the inviolable, immutable, and unmanifest law or eternal principle that governs the cosmos. All dynamic changes in the universe happen according to Allah but Allah remains invariant. A cat would not jump off a roof, as it is instinctively aware of the impact of gravitation. Allah governs the trajectory of your mind too, but unlike a cat, which depends on its innate intelligence, you are blinded by clever logic and stumble without knowing what is true and what is false and suffer the consequences. You would recognize the nature of Allah when you come out of this stupor and intuitively perceive reality as it is."

"Do prayers help?"

"Prayers are meant to keep the mind still and open the doors to your heart. Prayers are a way of expressing your gratitude and recognition of the compassionate and merciful Allah that nurtures abundant life in deep oceans, high mountains, and even in the arid Arabian desert," Muhammad responded. "It is like expressing your love for your mother who gave birth to you, took care of you, and has always wished you the very best in life. Allah is no different. Allah has given birth to you and will do everything that is good for you. When you realize this truth, you will lose fear and anxiety, be grateful for whatever Allah offers, and live in peace."

Abraham

I asked Abraham why he rejected all gods before Yhwh.

Abraham began, "I rejected gods of all prevailing religions when I realized that there is only one invariant and inviolable supreme principle from the beginning of time that is the same for all people. In the beginning was the Word, the Word was with God, and the Word was God. If you understand it, you would understand everything."

I could not make head or tail of what it meant, and I said so.

Abraham nodded and asked, "Yes, but what do you make of this statement anyway?"

"I could say with absolute certainty that I came first. I came even before the beginning and well before God," I responded. And after a brief pause added, "in the word, 'In'."

However, looking at the stern expression on his face, I quickly corrected my attitude and answered with due deference. "I presume that it relates to the beginning of creation, but I encounter three fundamental problems with this observation. The word 'beginning' begs the questions: What was there before the beginning? How did it begin? Who created it? They quickly turn into an infinite regression. I presume that the word 'word' must mean something special. Apparently, the word used in Hebrew was '*davar*,' which was translated into '*logos*' or principle in Greek, and eventually into 'word' in English. Finally, I have absolutely no clue what the word God really means. All I could conjecture is that the *Beginning* of creation, *Word*, and *God* are somehow inseparably connected to each other, like the three sides of the same coin."

"Quite so," responded Abraham, looking pleased, much to my profound relief, I might add. "I especially like the way you refer to it as three sides of the same coin. Most people ignore the lateral side (thickness) that binds and maintains the integrity of the coin, which is exactly the role of the principle or the laws of nature. Look at these words afresh from your current scientific perspective and resist the temptation to replace the unknown with myths. Let the unknown remain unknown until it is known. Be honest. Be patient. Be courageous. Let truth reveal itself.

"Creation is a mystery. Neither its beginning nor the end is known in either space or time. Whether there was a beginning or not is a moot point. Scientists believe that it started with the Big Bang. Obviously, you wouldn't be here without a beginning. What you could state with certainty is that dynamic interactions of matter and energy seem to be playing out on an empty platform or what one might call a zero substratum that extends to infinity in space and time. The cosmic drama is governed by an invariant and inviolable davar. The manifest *creation*, the invariant, invisible and inviolable *davar*, and *emptiness* (zero) are the three facets of the universe.

"The universe is governed by davar. It has no physical attributes, but its presence is indubitable. Thunder and lightning, the earth, the oceans, the sun, the moon, and the planets, and all the rest are governed by davar. And so are you. It is unmanifest, immutable, and inviolable, which is consistent with your definition of a scientific law."

"If it is a law of nature, why did you not simply call it a law, explain its characteristics, and be done with it, which could have saved all the confusion and turmoil?" I asked.

"I did not call it a law for two main reasons," Abraham responded. "Firstly, scientific laws were unknown during my time. Nature was a mystery, a *tabula rasa*. Secondly, people were aware of only the laws of the kings. I made sure that they did not mistake davar for the laws imposed by capricious rulers and priests based on moral, sin, reward, and punishment. I wanted people to know that davar was inviolable and no amount of sacrifices and image worship could change or mitigate the consequences of actions carried out in ignorance.

"I realized that the law that governs our life could be divided into two types. The first type consists of a law (or a set of laws) that governs the objective world of physical matter. The laws of physics, such as the law of gravitation, belong to the first group. It was unknown to us, but we knew what would happen if we jumped off a cliff. The second category governs the subjective or psychological world of emotions, which was our focus. What we discovered was not a common law that could be enforced in a court. It was also not an objective law of the physical world."

Abraham continued with his exposition, "Yhwh is not a supernatural God of the primitive people. It is emptiness on which the cosmic drama unfolds in accordance with davar. Yhwh is empty. It is the shunyata or emptiness of the Buddha. As emptiness cannot be described by images, I discouraged image worship. Since the law is invisible, I introduced the practice of precepts to become aware of the nature of the law and refrain from acting blindly.

"A sadistic God is not seeking eye-for-an-eye or tooth-for-a-tooth, but you are likely to trip and fall when you act blindly with false perceptions of reality. Davar cannot be violated as it has zero tolerance for errors. You could worship God and offer a sacrificial goat at the altar, but the result would still be the same if you jump off a cliff. Your body is healthy only within a narrow band such as homeostasis—I did not know the word then, but I knew the need for proper food habits. Deviation from it would lead to pain, suffering, and possibly death. Davar cannot be placated. Hence, I encouraged followers to become aware of davar and live in accordance with it. I also asked them to remain silent and become directly aware of the true nature of Yhwh."

Abraham said, "Yhwh is unmanifest. I forbade image worship because images are like the shadows or reflections in a mirror. People cling to their self-image (ego) as if life depends on it. It is as absurd as a dog chasing its own tail. *You don't have to cling to your ego, it clings to you, just like a shadow.* Your vain attempts to decorate it cause energy dissipation and suffering."

On hearing the word suffering, Buddha came out of his meditation to make it clear for the egghead. "There is no god but no-god; it is shunyata or nothing-ness There is no self but no-self; it is anatta. There is no mind but no-mind; it is nirvana. Emptiness and form are complementary; one cannot exist without the other. There is no-thing and that is everything you need to know."

He went back to *zazen*.

Others encouraged me to ask questions and seek clarifications. I started with an innocuous question about the universe that has always intrigued me, "What is beyond everything, beyond galaxies, black holes, space, and time?"

Abraham, whose name led all the rest, answered.

Everything and Nothing

"Beyond everything there is Nothing,"
Abraham asserted succinctly.
"Creation is everything plus Nothing,
A void that extends to infinity.
Governed by an Eternal Principle
Everything is dynamic and temporal
As it changes continuously,
Always seeking balance and symmetry.

But Nothing is Eternal and Invariant!
Lacking everything and yet complete,
Nothing is naturally balanced and free."
My head was swirling like an eddy
As Reality appeared topsy-turvy.
He asked me not to worry,
And comfortingly added,
There is Nothing in your head!

I certainly felt light knowing that there was nothing in my head. A Zen master might have asked me to get rid of nothing too.

Playing with words such as everything and nothing, emptiness and form, etc. meant little to a diehard skeptic like me, who prides in logical, rational, and critical thinking. What was the relevance of their esoteric observations? Were they trying to impress me with bombastic but empty mumbo-jumbo? I was interested in practical insights like *Seven Effective Steps to Nirvana*. So, I became pragmatic.

I sought the meaning of life, beginning from an ignorant childhood, gathering knowledge and skills to deal with the vagaries of life, trying to become rich, famous, and powerful, growing old, and finally ending up dead. For eons, every generation has been following the same routine. "What is the purpose of all these meaningless and seemingly endless activities?" I asked.

Laozi

"What would you consider purposeful or meaningful?" countered Laozi (Mitchell 2006) with a gentle smile, and asked, "Whether they are purposeful or pointless would depend on your frame of reference. In the absence of a uniformly valid and invariant frame of reference for your values, all answers turn out to be tautological. Questions on the meaning and purpose of life arise only when you are unhappy, when the mind clings to illusions, mistaking appearance for real.

"Such questions are irrelevant to an individual who is fearless, happy, playful, and creative. *It is more meaningful to ask yourself if it is worth living a fettered, fearful, and anxiety-ridden life of compromises.*

"You cannot obtain a unique answer using dualistic logic as long as you do not have a verifiable, absolute frame of reference that is invariant with people, place, and time. Religion, philosophy, science, ideology, etc. do not offer such a framework. Their values differ significantly from each other, often in a mutually exclusive manner. Wisdom that is based on linear, dualistic thinking, past experience, and social values literally leads you to a dead-end. Awareness of the true nature of reality would obliterate the question itself.

"Nature could be viewed as a quintessential narcissist, deeply in love with herself, trying to fulfill her curiosity through the human mind to admire and play with her amazing creation. Regardless of whether you call it a purpose or not, it is something that she seems to be really keen on, and for being innately playful and falling in love with her creation, she rewards you with peace and happiness. Who, with a sane mind, would refuse her!

"Brilliant philosophers like Kierkegaard, Nietzsche, Pascal, and others searched for truth with logic and reason but, sadly, they did not take the crucial step beyond the intellect to realize the true nature of their emotions, thereby missing *nirvana* by a whisker. Humanity would have immensely benefited from them if they had realized their innate nature. Instead of falling down to realize bliss, they climbed up the intellectual ladder to experience melancholy."

Laozi continued, "Those who take that extra step beyond the intellect will experience an ecstatic free fall into their innate center. The center is a point with no dimensions, but it is miraculously connected to the infinite, with an infinite number of lines radiating from it. It would be like dying to the old (self-image) and being born again as the real self or no-self. Only then does one get a glimpse of the true nature of infinite reality. When you are peaceful and blissful, you will find creative expression for your emotions."

I interrupted him as he tried to continue his spiel on stepping into the void beyond wisdom. "Climbing up and falling down, looking up and transcending intellect are words that mean nothing unless you provide practical examples to emulate. Instead of impractical teachings, inconvenient morals, and violent punishments for sins, why don't you give, without metaphors, parables, and analogies, a rigorous logical description of the nature of reality that you seem to hold in such high esteem? Why all this hocus-pocus?"

Laozi smiled sympathetically at my impudence but continued in his usual earnest and serene manner. "What we conveyed was simple and direct, but it appears complex and convoluted to your skeptical, cynical, and dualistic intellect that is habituated to linear thinking and associative logic. *We never spoke of morals, sins, crime, and punishment, which are the creations of your clergy and rulers.* You perceive two abstract images of the psychological world as good and evil and cling to one of them while ignoring the others, which cause fear, anxiety, and uncertainty.

"You become gullible when you are intoxicated by your cravings and self-image. You believe in childish superstitions and subscribe to inane rituals in your vain attempts to satisfy your desires. Theologians profess and you claim to have faith in avatars, messiahs, and prophets with direct contact with God but, if that were so, why do you not practice their precepts? You claim to have faith in them, but tell lies, steal, kill, and are avaricious!

"Everyone knows the risk of practicing the precepts and the teachings. Even a kid knows that it would not bring the material and social benefits that you crave. Children copy their parents who pay lip service in the church, mosque, synagogue, temple, etc. during the weekends but submit to their cravings during their *weak* days. Logical justifications are used to hide deception and hypocrisy. You wear masks that hide your true identity and agenda.

"*You need to unmask yourself to realize your true nature.* Others cannot do it for you. From being a person playing different roles in society, you must become your innate, individual self. Precepts and the teachings were not an exhortation to lead a moral life, but a guide to realize your innate nature. Instead of wearing the mask of a believer but lacking faith, you must have the courage to explore, experiment, and verify or falsify the precepts and teachings."

Pointing to an oak tree, Laozi continued, "I know that you loathe analogies, but if I were to tell a child that the giant oak tree grew from a tiny acorn, it might be viewed as hocus-pocus. The child cannot *see* the germination of the seed, sprouting of the plant, and the entire growth of the tree instantly demonstrated in front of it. Even you do not know how you emerged from a sperm and an egg and became what you are today, although you were innately involved in the entire process. Regardless of how brilliant you are, you cannot learn to swim merely by reading a swimming manual or by looking at fish in an aquarium. You have to get your feet wet, so to say.

"A child would never learn to read or write without practicing the wiggly and meaningless alphabets that are strung together to make words and sentences, where even blank space plays a crucial role. The teachings were meant for implementation because we knew that through practice, you'd eventually realize the truth that liberates. Instead, you converted them into a moral code to certify saints, sinners, and martyrs. You have invented myths to hide your ignorance. The precepts are not worth the stone tablet they are inscribed on if you do not practice them. You will understand their intended purpose only through practical experimentation."

I pointed out that I am, after all, an ordinary mortal and not divine. "I understand and admit to all these faults, but I constantly face danger from natural forces as well as other human beings. It is important for me to be logical, reasonable, and use critical thinking to question every concept, every teaching, every ideology, or doctrine before I implement them. I need verifiable evidence. I am skeptical but not closed minded."

"Besides," I continued with my self-defense, "application of logic and reason have led to spectacular progress in mathematics, science, and technology. We are able to correctly predict the existence and properties of sub-atomic matter merely through mathematical modeling and conjectures. We explore outer space without physically traveling to distant parts of the universe. We build machines to study our brains, fly across vast oceans, and enjoy luxuries that even the richest monarchs of yore could not have imagined.

"Today, children know how to use computers, which you never had. We have made big strides in creating a relatively free society where we can express our ideas without being tortured, exiled, burned, impaled, or killed. All these and more would have been impossible without a logical, rational, and ethical approach.

"Furthermore, I am aware of the tragedy that struck Jesus, Socrates, and others whose lives were cut short by insecure rulers and their henchmen. I do not fancy that happening to me. Tell me if you have some safer way to relate to, or experience, that which you hold so highly, without having to practice your impractical precepts and teachings."

Jesus

Jesus suddenly entered the fray with an admonition.

"Wow! So, you think that my teachings were impractical," he said. "Pray, tell me, what was my most important message? You could then enlighten me as to what is impractical about it."

I reeled off his Sermon on the Mount, which I thought was the most profound, but he rejected each part I mentioned. Finally, he himself answered the question.

"In fact," he said, "the most important message was not even a part of my sermon but it came right after it ended when I warned my disciples that those who merely heard what I said but did not practice what they heard are like a man who builds a house on sand. It will collapse like a house of cards when floods come or winds blow, and the destruction would be great. All the woes of Christianity can be attributed to the followers who did not faithfully practice what they'd heard. I asked them to practice the teachings, repent past mistakes, be forgiving, and not judge others. They did just the opposite: they were not faithful in practice, were remorseless, judged others, were vengeful, and used disingenuous justifications to carry out cruel deeds.

"It is deceptive to praise peace but spread violence, to promise freedom but enforce subservience, to extol forgiveness but seek revenge, to preach love and kindness but practice bigotry, to glorify meekness but grab power, and admire poverty but accumulate wealth," rebuked Jesus, and thundered, "You cannot be serious!" in a mock imitation of my favorite tennis maestro John McEnroe, as I bowed my head in embarrassment.

Jesus continued, "It is certainly pleasant to hear the sermons on weekends, smugly ride the high horse on weak days, and altogether ignore the teachings in practice. I was not unaware of the consequences and the likely hardships that you would face in practicing the teachings. I knew that it would expose your weaknesses. In fact, *the primary purpose of the teachings was to expose your weakness to you.*

"However, I also knew that your innate intelligence would naturally compel you to make efforts to overcome your weaknesses, become strong and guide you to truth and liberation. I had faith in you, but you seem to lack faith in yourself. Without faith in your innate nature, you are condemned to a life of fear and anxiety. Truth cannot be told. You can realize truth only through diligent practice of the teachings and not through the mere recitation of chapter and verse."

Jesus added, "The questions you must ask yourself are: *Does your life create music or headaches, is joyful or miserable, spreads fragrance or stinks, is free or fettered?*"

Jesus continued, "In the long run, nothing is safe. I am credited with bringing back Lazarus to life after he was dead. That is not factual but metaphorical. However, even if you believe that to be a fact, you must know that he is not alive today. So, he must have died again, and nobody saved him the second time. I certainly didn't. There is no escape from death. Birth and death are the beginning and end of a beautiful movement in an endless symphony of life.

"You should know that the people who nailed me on the cross are also dead as a doorknob. It was just a matter of time before they too died. You too will die someday. Birth gives rise to new life and through death nature recycles the old to a more evolved version. Once you get rid of your preoccupation with death, you will find the courage to seek truth, when even death will not deter you. If you were to ask the Buddha, he would tell you that *no-thing* is safe!"

"What about the actual suffering that I experience?" I persisted. Who knew whether I'd get another opportunity to hear from the horse's mouth!

The Buddha

The Buddha's ears perked up again on hearing the word suffering.

"Emotional discontent or suffering will end when mental wellbeing is restored," he said. "Some philosophers mistakenly portrayed me as a nihilist because I stated that life is characterized by suffering (*dukkha*). I followed a logical technique known as *reductio ad absurdum* or proof by negation of the absurd.

"For example, I stated that life is characterized by suffering as the first Noble Truth," the Buddha said. "I spent many years using associative logic to find the cause of suffering and failed, but it led to a paradoxical discovery. I found that life was indeed blissful. Absurdity is intuitively revealed when you are faced with a contradiction that cannot be resolved in a logical manner."

The Buddha continued, "My first Noble Truth alluded to suffering as a part of life. Before guiding people to a state where there is no suffering, I had to first acknowledge suffering as their actual experience. In stark contrast, my Fourth Noble Truth asserted that there was an eight-fold Noble Path to end suffering. If suffering is eliminated by practicing the eight-fold Noble Path, as it promised, then it would mean that life is not full of suffering after all. Thus, if the fourth Noble Truth stating that suffering could be ended were true, then the first Noble Truth stating that life is suffering must be false (absurd), a blatant lie and not a Noble Truth! The first and fourth Noble Truths cannot simultaneously be true. One of them is false. However, a logical path to verify the validity of my teachings does not exist. The only way to experience nirvana is through diligent practice. Jesus and I are in complete agreement on diligent practice!

"Brilliant philosophers have incorrectly concluded that I was nihilistic and that my teachings were life-negative because they did not experience nirvana. They fail to mention that they did not practice the eight-fold Noble Path either! After all, they might have applied associative logic to deduce from the first Noble Truth that life was a suffering and there was no point in reading further, since they were searching for happiness and were not interested in knowing more about suffering. They already knew enough about suffering from direct experience.

"In fact, Blaise Pascal, a brilliant 17th-century scientist and philosopher (Houston 1984), observed the widespread presence of suffering and concluded that happiness was an illusion and misery was the norm. His conclusion was based on associative logic and common sense, just as the perception of a stationary earth with orbiting celestial bodies is based on common sense. The fact that life is a celebration can be realized only by practicing precepts and teachings and not through intellectual argumentation."

"You gave an eight-fold Noble Path, but Krishnamurthy said that truth is a pathless land (Krishnamurthy 2003). Who is right?" I wondered loudly.

"Krishnamurthy is right, certainly, but you must ask him how he arrived at his conclusion! Arrival implies a path, does it not? Or, did an angel drop him there? He was intuitive. He was like an eagle urging eaglets to jump off their aerie and fly. They do not need lessons in flight mechanics. I was trying to guide people who were blindly stumbling on the ground."

I asked cheekily, "Did you ever experience suffering after attaining nirvana?"

He responded earnestly, "Let me respond with a question. Do you suffer because you cannot fly like a bird?"

"No, though I wish I could. Instead, we have invented aircraft to fly. As an aeronautical engineer, I enjoy working on solving problems to make it safer and more efficient. We are learning to build airplanes to fly-by-feel, like a bird. To answer your question, no, I do not suffer just because I cannot fly like a bird."

"Yes, I understand," responded the Buddha. "And, you have many limitations in sensing too. Animals surpass you in many sensing capabilities. You cannot outrun a cheetah, do thermal imaging like a snake, or ultrasonic echolocation like a bat, but you have invented technologies that extend your capabilities, many of which do not even have a parallel in nature. They are not the result of suffering but thanks to the ingenuity and playful curiosity of the human mind. Your limitations have been sublimated into creative expression.

"Your desire to excel in the arts, music, and sports requires discipline, hard work, and physical exertion, but you do not call it pain or suffering. You are excited by these challenges. Nature provides the energy and resources to joyfully express your creativity. You are not bogged down by challenges but invigorated by the opportunity."

"It would be so much more effective if you could provide a systematic, foolproof, step-by-step instruction manual to end ignorance and realize my innate nature," I ventured. "You did suggest an eight-fold Noble Path, or eight steps to nirvana, with each step starting with the word right as in right view, right thought, etc., but, being ignorant and used to dualistic thinking, I do not know what is right and what is wrong. Besides, there are New Age gurus at every street corner selling the 'rights' for a fee. Is there a manual on what is right? How do I identify right from wrong and good from evil?"

"First of all, let me correct you," responded the Buddha. "I did not use the word 'right.' Each step starts with the word *samma*, which means balance, equal, or same. It is used in the same sense that you balance a mathematical equation with a zero on the right-hand side. Your goal is to eliminate mental disturbances by eliminating *discord among feelings, thoughts, words, and actions*, i.e., by making discord equal to zero at each step. However, I will answer your question as if I'd used the word right. It does not alter the essence of the approach.

"It is impossible to uniquely differentiate dualistic values such as right from wrong, good from evil, etc. without a uniformly valid frame of reference that is invariant with people, place, or time," the Buddha said. "All the values that you subscribe to are invariably man-made and vary with race, ethnicity, culture, tribe, religion, ideology, etc. They also change from one generation to another. On the other hand, an emotion that emerges naturally is not dualistic but absolute. Like hunger and thirst, you know it with absolute certainty and without external authority. The feeling of hunger has not changed in a million years. And everyone feels it.

"I gave thousands of sermons in over four decades to clarify my teachings. Vimalakirti, a wealthy businessman, a lay follower, and benefactor, was an unexpected and unsolicited accomplice who shocked my senior disciples with dualistic obfuscations to awaken them from a logical nightmare. But that is a long story. I would be happy to narrate it some other time. Although my disciples adored me and intellectually agreed with me, they remained unaware of their ignorance caused by a dualistic interpretation of my teachings. He questioned them with logically valid contrarian views. In the Christian and Muslim lexicon, Vimalakirti was indulging in blasphemy and heresy right under my nose but with my enthusiastic and tacit approval!"

"What is right?" I persisted.

"It is *right* when *your feelings, thoughts, words, and actions are in harmony*," the Buddha said. "You must remember that the word right is absolute and not relative. Jesus said truth liberates but he too did not define truth because it is absolute.

"In fact, it is far more important to know what is wrong or false because falsehood is easily recognized, and *truth* is naturally revealed when all falsehood is exposed and eliminated. I shall describe wrong in a way that you could directly and unmistakably recognize it as a fact.

"It is wrong when your *feelings, thoughts, words, and actions are not in accord with each other and with your innate emotions.* You experience freedom only when they are in harmony. Any discord among them creates fear, anxiety, disturbance, unhappiness, uncertainty, etc. within the mind. This discord is associated with energy dissipation that is experienced as suffering. When reality does not meet your expectations, it leads to a new cycle of fear and anxiety. The cycle is interspersed with a few respites, but it is always resumed with a new cycle of desires and expectations. You are trapped in this rut, the wheel of life (*samsara chakra*). You need to break free from this cycle that is running out of control like a runaway locomotive.

"This discord within one's own mind is ultimately what is *wrong*. The challenge is to identify the source of discord and eliminate it. It is something that only you can do because the discord is within you. Only you know if you have a stomachache and you feel the pain quite clearly.

"You could begin with simple experiments to realize that the mind is harmonious, peaceful, and balanced when your feelings, thoughts, words, and actions are aligned with each other. Commitment and consistent effort are required to maintain equanimity in the face of adversity, which would eventually lead to the natural state of nirvana or no-mind.

"Progress would be rapid in a society with normal human interactions, but it is fraught with risk. I established the *sangha* or monastery to facilitate the practice in a safe and healthy surrounding. Once cured of mental afflictions, the realized ones (*Bodhisattvas*) went into the open to help others.

"Zarathustra was, perhaps, the first to emphasize the importance of good thoughts (*humata*), good words (*hukhta*), and good deeds (*huvarshta*) (Kapadia 1905). Of course, he too did not define what was good in unequivocal language. I merely extended his three-fold precept to an eight-fold Noble Path by including right *view* or attitude as the first requirement. If everyone practiced his simple three-fold teaching, the world would be peaceful, playful, and creative."

I was puzzled. "You say that there is no logical path to nirvana and yet you are asking me to follow the path you have described. Do I need to have faith in your teachings? How do I choose the right direction since every path has two diametrically opposite directions?"

"You may follow Yogi Berra," the Buddha replied with a captivating smile. "'When you come to a fork on the road, take it!' Jokes aside, it is right *when your feelings, thoughts, words, and actions are aligned with your emotions.* Of course, you may not be able to realize it immediately. You may encounter many obstacles on the path. It is more important and relatively more straightforward to recognize what is wrong and eliminate it. I spent nearly six years to eliminate all the internal contradictions. It is an iterative process until all contradictions suddenly disappear, and you intuitively realize your innate nature. It follows the modern scientific principles of active control of dynamic systems with negative feedback (Franklin 1994).

"Scientific discoveries also occur suddenly, in an intuitive manner. By the very nature of things, there is no logical procedure to discover an unknown phenomenon. Millions may have watched ripe apples fall down from trees, but it took the brilliance and diligence of Newton to see something profound in that seemingly simple phenomenon. He also saw that heavenly bodies kept orbiting without falling out of the sky. He related these phenomena to gravitation and forces of attraction and repulsion pulling the bodies in opposite directions. He described balance with his third law, which states that action and reaction are equal and opposite. Curiosity and earnest application of his mind led to great discoveries.

"Great or small, the discovery of a hitherto unknown phenomenon always occurs intuitively, as a result of diligent experimentation, but there is no guarantee that a discovery will take place. However, it is a relatively simple matter to logically describe the path that led to the discovery.

"You are the laboratory where you explore your mind. Unlike a scientific discovery, which is objective and becomes common knowledge, nirvana is subjective. *Nobody can discover the nature of your mind for you.* You have no choice but to do it yourself. You learn through trial and error. You might call that faith or commitment.

"Discoveries in the objective world are made once but nirvana is discovered afresh by every individual. It is not a discovery of a new phenomenon but the recognition of an illusion, like a ghost in the lamppost! How do you logically discover something that does not exist?

"Billions of dollars were spent to build super-accelerators in part to verify the existence of what has been named as a god particle, the Higgs-Boson, based on scientific predictions and mathematical modeling (Lederman 2013). It led to the discovery of the particle that is assumed to exist, but what I am suggesting is even more baffling because the self that does not exist can be discovered! It is a great challenge to describe the discovery of something that does not exist! Why don't you conduct an experiment just the way you went after Higgs-Boson?

"*I am not asking you to have faith. It is your call, your freedom to decide. It costs nothing, and you will find no-thing!*"

The Buddha then gently changed the topic, "You may justifiably complain that my sermons are long, abstract, require introspection and meditation over long periods of time, and promise *no-thing* at the end, and that you do not have the time or patience. In stark contrast, Jesus's sermons are brief, unambiguous, and positive assertions that are so simple that even a child could understand them. You encounter numerous opportunities every day to practice his teachings, but you ignore them. You claim that he gave up his life to save you. What excuse do you have for having little faith in Jesus, the most compassionate man to ever walk on earth (water)?"

I had no excuse other than to admit to a lack of faith in his teachings and a lurking doubt that Jesus probably had no clue about my real difficulties. "I cannot survive in an adversarial social order if I practiced his teachings. I would end up as a doormat and become fodder for my enemies. My biological instincts compel me to fight for my survival and to kick the rear of my perceived enemies. I am aware of what happened to Jesus himself. Even he is presumed to have wondered on the cross, why his Abba in heaven had forsaken him. However, as the Son of God he might have resurrected himself, but I do not have that luxury. For me, it is a one-way ticket into oblivion. How can I practice his teachings with confidence? What guarantees do I have?"

Krishna

"You are more afraid of pain, suffering, and death than you care to admit," Krishna interjected. "You quote Patrick Henry, *'Give me liberty or give me death,'* and as a believer in Jesus you expect to go to heaven after death, but you let others fight and die for you while you and your loved ones hide in the bunkers. You give posthumous awards and medals as if they are of any value to the dead people. They are a pyrrhic consolation to those who have lost their dear ones. You use drones that maim and kill unarmed women and children and call it collateral damage. Where is your humanity, your compassion? Your claim to be a follower of Jesus is bogus. You are ever ready with a logical excuse to justify violence and cruelty. If you honestly believe in a just cause, lead from the front, and fight with courage. Sniping from behind Jesus's coattails is a cowardly and dastardly act."

Krishna continued to chide me. "Insecurity, falsehood, ignorance, cowardice, deception, and violence go together. They create mortal fear of those whose presence exudes fearlessness, truth, and freedom. Albert Camus observed, *"The only way to deal with an unfree world is to become so absolutely free that your very existence is an act of rebellion"* (Camus 1956).

"Neither Muhammad nor I shied away from a good fight when all attempts at peace failed to persuade those who were intent on bringing harm to those who desired peace. Muhammad freed slaves, which did not go well with the priests and rulers of Mecca, who persecuted him and his followers for over a decade (Armstrong 1992). His life was threatened when his wife Khadijah and influential uncle Abu Talib died. He fled to Yathrib (Medina) to escape further persecution but they chased him there too. Finally, this middle-aged merchant, with no military training, routed the professional Meccan army and brought peace without shedding any further blood."

"Jesus was loving and kind while the Buddha led a life of a mendicant, but Muhammad and I were not averse to taking to arms to prevent evil," Krishna continued. "The best solution is to be strong enough to scare the daylights out of those who even dream of harming others; be gentle toward the rest, protect the vulnerable; and try utmost to avoid violence.

"The Vedic Rishis conveyed a pithy four-fold approach for conflict resolution: *Saama dhaana bheda dandam.* Begin with a peaceful, equitable, and balanced approach (*saama*). If it does not work, make a generous offer (*dhaana*) that is difficult to refuse. If that too fails, find reconciliation through discussions and negotiations (*bheda*). Only when all these attempts at conflict resolution fail, and the other is intent on harming, use the stick (*danda*) as a final resort."

Krishna then dealt me a decisive blow. "You have become adept at giving logical excuses, providing disingenuous justifications, and offering reasoned arguments to negate everything we conveyed. You sing our praise and put us on a pedestal to worship but do not practice our teachings. It shows that you have neither faith in us nor respect for our intelligence.

"Your claim to religious faith is a façade. You do it to divert attention from your hidden agenda. Your actions are not based on love or faith in Jesus and his teachings but driven by fear of pain, suffering, and death. Your craving for fame, wealth, power, and legacy is an attempt to divert your attention from your fear of death. You have become a coward and cowards can never be free. Freedom comes from courage, as Thucydides said two millennia ago."

Krishna brought me back to my senses. I stepped down from my high horse.

I confessed, "I realize my cowardice, but I lack the clarity to overcome the hurdles that I encounter in my daily life. I need help and guidance to regain the courage to be honest. I feel stuck where I face a constant battle between the crippling social environment and the desire for liberation. You helped Arjuna on the battlefield of the great Kurukshetra war. Many things have changed since then. The world is scientifically, technologically, socially, economically, and politically far more advanced, and yet the emotional problems that I face are not different. Precepts and teachings are attractive, but I am unable to practice them in an adversarial social order. Also, atheistic ideologies have little to offer for emotional fulfillment. Their ethical principles also do not have a uniformly valid and invariant frame of reference. How do I resolve these mental conflicts and experience peace?"

Krishna became more sympathetic in response to my humble request. "Yes, times have changed. During my time, people were less informed and less knowledgeable, but many were innocent. Today, you are better informed, more knowledgeable, extraordinarily clever and deceptive, but emotionally unfulfilled. You have developed prejudices and values based on race, religion, gender, skin color, wealth, power, fame, education, and even where one lives. It is so noisy inside your brain that any attempt on my part to guide you tends to fall on deaf ears.

"In the *Bhagavad Gita* (Fosse 2007), I metaphorically exhibited my innate nature with the brightness of several thousand suns. Even Oppenheimer remembered that verse when he first saw the atomic bomb explode under the Manhattan Project. Today, if I were to express anything close to what I did then, you would disinterestedly walk away from me, uttering, 'Bah,' like your mentor Werner who used to dismiss those who did not make aerodynamic sense. The words faith and religion have become repulsive to you because of their association with hypocrisy, bigotry, and violence. The original meaning of religion or yoga was to bind together or unify but, sadly, organized religions have done the exact opposite, creating divisions."

"So, what can I say that would make sense to you?" Krishna asked rhetorically. "Absolutely nothing. Liberation is a subjective experience. However, since you asked, I would suggest that you seek the guidance of Patanjali. His

Ashtanga Yoga Sutra is well suited for the modern age. Patanjali was rational, systematic, and secular. He followed the scientific principles of passivity-based control of dynamic systems. At present, the focus of yoga may be on physical exercises, but the real purpose of yoga is to restore mental balance and emotional wellbeing.

"Patanjali's *Ashtanga Yoga Sutra* is to religion what Euclid's *Elements* is to mathematics (Fitzpatrick 2008). Euclid systematically compiled advanced theorems and their corollaries in analytical geometry based on axioms and mathematical knowledge that existed in Greece at his time. Patanjali compiled his Octad based on the existing understanding of the mind in India. His approach is rational, logical, and verifiably beneficial. I referred to it as the Royal Path, as it is independent of external authority. Seek his guidance."

I did.

Patanjali

Patanjali emerged from meditation to talk to me. "It is strange that human beings are, perhaps, the only species that practices self-deception. Of course, you wouldn't indulge in self-deception if you knew it. Suffering is the result of actions carried out in ignorance. It is like blindly falling into a ditch. To eliminate suffering, you must open your (inner) eyes, be aware of your innate nature, and cease this foolish habit of self-deception. *Ashtanga Yoga Sutra* is a systematic manual for self-inquiry to regain mental balance and self-awareness."

"The fundamental cause of self-deception," Patanjali explained, "is an *illusory perception that you are apart from the rest of nature and that it is possible to deceive others without deceiving yourself in the process.* Self-deception will disappear when you become reunited with nature and realize that any attempt to deceive others is the same as deceiving yourself, that it is like cutting your nose to spite the face. The goal of yoga is to end ignorance, restore balance (*samadhi*), and experience liberation, when you begin to naturally care for every living being just as you care for yourself. Compassion is natural when you are liberated."

"I feel pain when I have stomachache or injury but not when others experience them," I countered. "Does it not prove that I am quite separate from others? How could I ever believe otherwise? What is the real source of self-deception?"

Patanjali explained, "It is true that, at a gross level, you do not feel the pain experienced by another person. You may also not feel the mental suffering others go through. However, when your loved one suffers from a disease you do not experience the pain itself but feel pangs that arise from empathy. Even your pets seem to understand when you are suffering. You are connected at a subtle level that could be realized with a sensitive mind or *no-mind*.

"Time plays a critical role. Self-deception is masked by the time-delay between perceived cause and effect. There is a long time-gap between sowing a seed and a fully mature tree, but they are intimately connected. You sow the seed of your own future. As you sow so you reap. A logical explanation for how self-deception occurs does not exist. If it did, there would be no self-deception. It is generally recognized only *ex post facto*.

"I could say with absolute certainty that you would not be experiencing mental suffering today if you had not deceived yourself in the past. Your perception of reality was obviously flawed because you would have acted differently if you had known the consequences earlier. It is exactly as Socrates observed, *'nobody errs knowingly and willingly'* (Segvic 2000). The 'error' is revealed later but the fundamental cause is self-deception or ignorance. You might believe that others deceived you but in reality, you deceived yourself into trusting those by whom you feel deceived. You probably hoped to gain something by trusting them. You had the freedom not to trust others. It was your decision that turned foul. Your perception of reality was flawed."

"Please, tell me, how do I get out of this mire?" I pleaded.

Patanjali closed his eyes momentarily before responding, *"First and foremost, of course, you must take complete responsibility for all your thoughts, feelings, words (promises), and actions, and whole-heartedly accept the consequences."*

"It is the first of the Buddha's eight-fold Noble Path, balanced attitude or view (*samma ditti*). You have to depend on yourself, as you do not have access to reliable external data to verify and validate your assumptions and models. You are your own laboratory. Through diligent practice, you will eventually see the connection between the acorn and the oak tree, how you sowed the seed of your own future.

"In early childhood you sowed two types of seeds in your brain based on your perceptions. Your parents, siblings, friends, relatives, and 'others' caused different emotions within you. Some were positive and some negative. Some were rewards and others were punishments. You nurtured the positive seeds with emotions like love, trust, kindness, compassion, etc. They created healthy fruits in your relationship.

"You also sowed seeds that you nurtured with emotions like fear, suspicion, hatred, animosity, etc. They created fruits that cause suffering. However, both seeds are within you and both trees have grown within you. Both the tree of knowledge and the tree of life are within your mind. All your biases, bigotry, and animosity toward others are fruits borne out of the seeds you planted and nurtured in your own brain. In many people, the trees nurtured with negative emotions have taken deep roots and spread wildly out of control. They also tend to stunt the growth of trees nurtured with positive emotions or kill them entirely.

"Well-meaning gurus and psychologists may suggest that you must control your anger, hatred, fear, and similar negative emotions. It is like pruning a tree. They will grow again with a vengeance. You must find the root cause of the problem and completely eradicate it.

"*It takes three steps to eradicate self-deception.*

"The first step is to recognize that the toxic plant exists within. The second step is to recognize the nature of the plant and how it has been nurtured. The third step is to completely starve the plant of any nutrition. If these three steps are diligently carried out, the plant would naturally atrophy and die.

"You will find that it is your self-image that you have sown and nurtured. It is the image that must be starved of attention. Do it and you will eventually be free."

I wanted to know the purpose of yoga. "Hatha yoga has become popular in the West. What is the relevance of physical postures?"

"Asanas or hatha yoga is a body-centric approach with physical benefits," responded Patanjali. "It is essential preparation for your journey to mental balance. *Ashtanga Yoga Sutra** creates balance in the entire body-emotion-mind system to realize samadhi.

"The eight limbs of yoga could be divided into three stages: precepts, self-inquiry, and practice. The aim of precepts is to maintain a clean environment for the body and mind. Self-inquiry includes physical exercise (hatha yoga), breathing exercise (*pranayama*) as a feedback monitor of emotion, introspection with internal focus (*pratyahara*), concentration with external

---

* Chapter 7 on **Exploration** provides a rational explanation of the eight limbs *of Ashtanga Yoga Sutra*.

focus (*dharana*), and meditative practice (*dhyana*) to realize mental balance and *samadhi*.

"Samadhi or mental balance occurs instantly and unexpectedly at the end of diligent practice of *dhyana*. The third stage could be viewed as a *no-stage* where an intuitive transformation happens, just as suddenly as when a child first experiences physical balance to freely ride a bicycle. A moment earlier she was fearful, wobbly, and falling, but all of a sudden, she learns to freely enjoy the ride. We have the innate skills to swim or ride a bike, but only those who train diligently learn. Similarly, only those who diligently practice would realize samadhi. It is natural, as the intuition that is necessary to regain mental balance is innate to every human being."

Patanjali added, "I did not elaborate on how the transformation to samadhi takes place because it would be like explaining how the child suddenly realized the ability to physically balance herself and began to freely ride the bike. It is far easier to just do it."

"We have training wheels to help a child intuitively realize physical balance to ride a bicycle. Are there similar tools available to achieve mental balance?" I enquired.

Patanjali answered positively. "The teachings of the Buddha, Jesus, and Muhammad could greatly facilitate the dramatic transformation. The practice of the teachings paradoxically creates balance in cognitive functions and keep the mind centered. They are like the training wheels used by a child to learn bike-riding. Diligent practice of the teachings would guide an individual to intuitively attain mental balance, which is a sudden and spontaneous subjective experience."

I still had one more question. "It is not easy to recognize the true meaning of the teachings and, besides, many of them have been distorted and doctored by vested interests. Is there a self-help guide that I could understand and practice without external help?"

"Certainly," Patanjali responded. "Ask Zarathustra about it."

I profusely thanked Patanjali and headed for Zarathustra.

Zarathustra

Zarathustra is an individual whose imprints could be found in every religion, both Abrahamic and Eastern. According to legends, he was a rare baby who was born laughing. I had no problem tracking him. If you hear loud laughter and people holding on to their stomach in pain from laughing, you could be certain that Zarathustra must be around. If you have a serious problem, he is the go-to-guy. He will show you how much worse it could be and make you feel good about your current problem.

I began with the question that had long puzzled me. "I cannot obtain a unique understanding of religious precepts and teachings with dualistic logic. The sixth commandment says, 'You shall not kill,' but millions have been killed in wars by the followers of Abrahamic religions. Millions of innocent animals are butchered every day for food. How can one type of killing be right and the other wrong? Muhammad and Krishna indulged in violence, whereas the Buddha and Jesus extolled non-violence. How can both be right? Please, help."

"It is a perennial question," answered Zarathustra seriously. "It is impossible for you to define right and wrong without a uniformly valid and invariant frame of reference for your dualistic values. But you don't have such a reference. You tend to look for justifications and excuses to defend your actions. Animals don't feel the need to logically defend themselves or apologize for their actions. They do not glorify their pack members with medals for killing their own species in combat. Only human beings feel the need for recognition and logical explanations for deception because of the perceived need for social status and to protect social capital.

"Portraying a nation as an evil enemy gives the group members the justification to kill the perceived enemies who are completely unknown to them. Samuel Johnson, a pioneer of the English Dictionary said, *Patriotism is the last refuge of the scoundrel'* (Boswell 2008). Although killing a single person within the group is considered a criminal act, it is, however, considered right and even glorious to kill thousands of those branded as enemies. The former gets a lethal injection and the latter gets a medal. Right and wrong, good and evil, etc., are values that vary with people (society), place, and time. This much you already know and seem to have reconciled with it. So, what really is your question?"

"I need to know the absolute truth." I said. "Anything less, is already available and quite unsatisfactory. It is a silly game that everyone seems to be playing for God knows what reason. I am not interested in self-deception or in deceiving others. Is there a practice that leaves no doubt in my mind that I am on the right track?"

"Of course, there is a practice," Zarathustra assured me with a straight face. "It will cost you money."

Roaring with laughter on seeing my face grow darker, he continued, "I was just kidding. There is a practice that does not depend on scriptures, morals, or the sanction of an external authority. That absolute authority is within you!"

I was puzzled. "The very fact that I am asking you indicates that I am depending on you, but you are saying that the authority is within me. Am I not accepting that on your authority? Please, do not tease me with these riddles. Please, show me the way."

It took a while for Zarathustra to stop laughing. He seemed to have no concern for my predicament, but it would have taken someone more than a laughing Zarathustra to escape without answering my question. I would have chased him down to the ends of the world if I believed that he had the answer. And he seemed to understand that he was dealing with a stubborn customer. He stopped laughing and gave me a simple and beautiful answer.

With sparkling eyes, he said, "In *Bhagavad Gita*, Krishna convinced Arjuna by revealing his divine form with a brightness of a thousand suns. Arjuna accepted that as proof for the divine nature of Krishna and trusted whatever he said without understanding anything. People have been quoting this farcical exhibition forever. Even Oppenheimer quoted this theatrical behavior when he witnessed the explosion of the first atom bomb. I do not use such gimmicks. In fact, I would give you a foolproof solution that even you can understand (*thanks!*) You will not need me anymore, as I too am equally eager to be free of your interminable questions.

"Listen! What you need to do is quite simple. You need to make sure that your *humata, hukhta, and huvarshta* (good feelings, good thoughts, and good deeds) (Kapadia 1905) are always aligned with your emotions. Any dissonance among them is a sure indication of the presence of internal contradictions that makes you suffer. When they are in consonance, you'll experience resonance with nature, which will reveal the truth that liberates. *Humata, hukhta, and huvarshta* create the dynamics that need to be balanced. It is similar to how a child balances counter-acting forces of gravitation, bicycle dynamics, and biomechanics to ride a bicycle.

"When your feelings, thoughts, words, actions, and emotions are in discord, the falsehood is within you. It happens when you cling to a world of illusions and compromise truth for gaining some perceived benefit from the society or external sources. Nietzsche observed—isn't it strange that I should quote a person whose best-known work is on me (Nietzsche 1999)!— *People don't want to hear the truth because they don't want their illusions shattered*

(Pippin 2012).' Before coming to any conclusion with a conditioned and afflicted mind, it is best to first understand the role of emotions and how they impact your mind.

"If you have lived a life of compromises, you will face many hurdles along the way because your friends and enemies have certain expectations of your politically correct and socially acceptable behavior. When you achieve harmony among feelings, thoughts, words and actions with diligent practice, your life will produce the right kind of music. When they are not in harmony, you will produce noise that first gives you a headache and then to others. Whether they are synchronized or not is known only to you and nobody else.

"You are the only authority to maintain harmony or accept dissonance. Explore, experiment and try to *maintain feelings, thoughts, words, and actions in harmony* (the second principle of *Debugging the Mind*) until you do not even have to think about them, as your response becomes spontaneous and natural. You are then free to express yourself through creativity and playfulness. Nature playfully expresses herself through you. It is the truth that will liberate you. It is the only practice that is needed. There is no other Truth."

That was it. He kept it simple and uncomplicated. There was no need for scriptures, God, morals, priests, rituals, prayers, worship, science, philosophy, ideology, no nothing. Liberation or nirvana is not a search for some esoteric or unknown truth. It is not an attainment but shedding of what we already have, viz., falsehood or discord among *feelings, thoughts, words, and actions*. When we lose all falsehood (discord), we realize harmony, just as Jesus said: "when you lose everything (false), you gain everything (the truth that liberates)."

Before bidding good-bye, I wished to take a selfie with them, when I suddenly remembered that they were supernatural beings who performed miracles. I wanted to verify if there was any truth to their legendary skills and, hopefully, videotape them for posterity.

"Do you guys perform miracles?" I asked, gripped with excitement and anticipation.

"No!" they responded in unison and vanished.

2

Journey in Search of My Self

I grew up in a well-educated middle-class family in India. My aim in life was to make enough money to play sports, be creative, and enjoy warm relationships with family and friends. I was not concerned about God, what happens after death, etc. Social status, wealth, and fame were of little interest to me. I saw life as a playground for having fun, but my playful attitude constantly got me and others into trouble.

I received a master's degree in aeronautical engineering, joined the faculty of the Indian Institute of Technology, Bombay (IITB) when I was twenty-three and married Bhavani, the girl I loved. I went to the Soviet Union on a faculty-exchange program and obtained a Ph.D. from Moscow State University. I became the father of two lovely girls and a cute boy. After working a dozen years at IITB, I came to the US as a senior post-doctoral fellow to do research at NASA.

Within a week of coming to the United States, I felt that I had come home. I fitted right in as I found people to be open, generous, cheerful, fearless, and conscientious.

I received unstinted support from my technical monitor, Ray, who was five years younger than me. Although he came from a Bible-thumping racist region of North Carolina, he was, like me, an atheist. Our research collaboration led to several NASA awards and papers at national and international aerospace conferences. We became close friends and went on camping and skiing trips with our families. He was a fun-loving guy. It was hard to get his attention when a pretty girl passed by. He had a great sense of humor. He once hung his briefs (underwear) on the bulletin board that was meant for weekly briefs! We both enjoyed unbridled laughter.

I recall overhearing a loud conversation Ray had with the branch secretary who asked him, "Hey, Ray, you are a redneck from North Carolina and Siva is from far-away India, from a completely different culture. How do you two get along so well, laughing all the time?"

His response still reverberates in me. He said, "Lori, Siva does not give a damn what I think of him, and I know what he thinks of me doesn't amount to a hill of beans. So, we get along quite fine!" How wonderful and liberating! Neither was bothered by what others thought of us.

Dr. Werner Pfenninger, my mentor, was almost twice my age at that time. He had a pronounced Swiss-German accent that many found difficult to understand, but I found him much easier to follow compared to the southern drawl of others at the Research Center. As he also tended to be brusque toward those who did not meet his high technical standards, NASA management was happy to let me work with him, which was good for me. I had him all to myself. I was, perhaps, the only person who took liberties with him and made him laugh.

Werner was an Evangelical Christian. When he tried to evangelize me, I frankly told him that I did not subscribe to any religion. He took it in the right spirit, as he had a soft spot for me. He and his spouse were happy to visit our family and have vegetarian dinner. He treated me like his own son, or even better. Once on a trip to Hawaii to attend a conference, we shared a room with another young scientist. Due to jetlag, I slept early on a pull-out bed without setting up the third bed. The young scientist complained to me the next morning that he'd slept on the floor, as Werner would not allow him to disturb me when I was fast asleep.

I was like a kid in a candy shop at NASA. The fantastic support that I received from the management enabled me to rapidly make valuable contributions. I was a foreigner with a Ph.D. from the bitter cold-war rival, the Soviet Union, but NASA treated me as its own. I even had free access to the best photographic equipment that allowed me to take pictures of the flow past one of my airfoils, which was published in a book (Hubin 1992).

Although I was a foreign national with a temporary visa and not a NASA employee, I was one of the select few who NASA took on a whirlwind tour of major aircraft companies like Boeing, Lockheed, McDonnell-Douglas, Northrop-Grumman, and others, in part to showcase my innovations. A derivative of a family of airfoils that I designed with the guidance of Werner (Mangalam and Pfenninger 1984) with unsurpassed aerodynamic performance (Selig 2003), was used in the wing design of Global Hawk RQ-4, a long-range, long-endurance, military aircraft (NASA-TechBrief 2010) built by Northrop-Grumman for the USAF, that won the coveted Collier Trophy, US aviation's highest honor. My innovations were highlighted in NASA annual reports for several years. One of my experiments using laser velocimetry was shown on the National Geographic TV channel. I was riding high.

I mentored high-school students under the Virginia Governor's New Horizons Program. I received a certificate of appreciation from the mayor of the city of Hampton for my community services on racial integration. I collaborated with several researchers, guided graduate students, and worked on a number of research projects above and beyond my job description.

Sports was my first love. I represented my post-graduate institute in cricket and tennis. I captained the Osmania university chess team. I played against chess masters at Moscow State University, but I was strongly discouraged from playing chess by my thesis adviser, who asked me to focus on my Ph.D. research. Soon after coming to the U.S., I became a certified USTA umpire and did line umpiring for tennis greats like Tracy Austin, Bjorn Borg and John McEnroe. I live in a resort area with plenty of sports facilities. When my tennis buddies would ask me when I was going to retire, my response was always: "I retired when I received a college degree. I have been playing ever since." I have found that playing sports promotes a balanced life.

At the end of my tenure as a senior post-doctoral fellow, I continued my research at NASA, first as an adjunct professor at Old Dominion University, and later as an independent contractor. I was happy for Ray when he was promoted as a manager and was delighted when he received the prestigious Floyd Thompson fellowship. However, when he left on a long study leave to do his Ph.D., and Werner left the group due to differences with the division chief, their absence caused me unforeseen problems that caught me off guard and threw me off balance.

I was vilified and thrown under the bus by those who were jealous of the rapid rise of Ray in the management, especially since he was an atheist. Some openly complained that Ray was promoted above his seniors because of my influence. One of them commented that I was spoilt by Ray. I laughed and said that I was independently *bad* even before I met him! My playful response didn't go well. He spread rumors that I was a Soviet agent. I was told that he came to the office with a gun but had been escorted out of NASA by security personnel before he could do any damage. I could not understand why I was being treated so poorly; I was friendly, had treated everyone with respect, and wished them well.

The electronic technician with whom I had patents and publications ostracized me. The irony was that I had seen him as a creative person who had not received due recognition from NASA, and I had naively tried to set the record straight. As he lacked expertise in aerodynamics, I wrote every word in the patent application and technical paper that described our discovery in flow physics. I had taken the initiative of making him the first author. I felt that it was an appropriate way to acknowledge his initiative and expertise in electronic sensors which led to the discovery. As a happy camper, I was not concerned about personal credit; I was only interested in being a part of a strong NASA research team.

I never understood what made him turn against a friend and well-wisher. We had no contact for over twenty years until I received a message from my former branch head that he was terminally ill and that he wanted to see me. He was unable to speak when I saw him, but without uttering a word he let me know how he felt. I wished him well. That was the last time I saw him.

I saw no point in working in a hostile environment. I wrote a brief "Thank you" note to Don, the branch head, and abruptly left without bidding any-one good-bye. I later came to know that the upper management viewed my decision to leave without consulting them as being disrespectful. I now realize that I could have handled it differently, especially since they were so support-ive of me. At that time, I had not wished to bother them with what I had thought were my personal problems, but, unfortunately, they felt slighted. I was blackballed.

I decided to obtain research contracts for the minority-owned high-tech business that I represented and focus on research opportunities under the highly competitive Small Business Innovation Research (SBIR) Program. I developed innovative technologies that brought over a couple of million dollars to the company and built a strong reputation among aerospace organizations, both in the US and abroad. I played a key role in transforming the two-man start-up company that was run from an attic into a multimillion-dollar company with well over 100 employees within three years. The company received the highest award from the Small Business Administration in recognition of these achievements.

But what I subsequently faced in the company shook me to the core.

When I was still on a temporary visa and doing research at NASA as an adjunct professor at Old Dominion University, the company owner, who also came from the same part of India where I am from, invited me to join his high-tech start-up business, promising me equal partnership when I became a US citizen. He already had another scientist as a partner. It was a gentlemen's agreement among the three of us who were conducting research in three different fields (aeronautics, structures, and materials) at NASA. As I was seen as a valuable asset, the company even had a huge key-person life insurance on me to protect its business interests. However, he reneged on the promise when I became a US citizen. He deceived the other partner also, who left the company in disgust, and joined NASA civil service. Being naïve and trusting, I had not taken adequate legal steps to protect my interests. It was a devastating blow.

Around this time, Ray suddenly died due to cardiac arrest. Werner was stricken with Parkinson's disease. I was blindsided by events over which I had no control. I was sad, middle-aged, and clueless. From being a high-flyer, I had a free fall like Icarus.

The problems that I encountered were not caused by people who were poor, but by those with an impoverished mind. Their wealth and social status were far above average, but they were being driven by base emotions like fear, jealousy, hatred, greed, covetousness, etc. I did not hate anyone or wish anyone harm. I was keen on figuring out how I was blind enough to be deceived, exploited, and hurt by so many people.

It was a time when my teenage kids needed my guidance and support. My wife had a major surgery. I too had health problems that required minor surgery. As I was going through this turmoil, I suddenly recalled a strange incident that had occurred a few years earlier while I was playing tennis. It had a huge impact on my life, which eventually led to this book.

I could not put away a simple volley at the net after maneuvering into a great position to win the point. What stopped me on my tracks was a strange thought about my father that hit me like a bolt of lightning and shook me up. I had always thought of him as a loser, with no street smarts, because, as a kid, I could not afford to play my favorite sport like cricket that required expensive gear. He used to invoke God and said that God would take care of all my needs. I thought that it was a weak cop-out to hide his inability to provide desired resources for me. I told him that I would never be like him when I grew up. He laughed and proudly told his friends that, unlike him, I would be smart and be materially well-off.

I suddenly realized on the tennis court, what an innocent person my father was and how true he was to his emotions. I had never heard or seen him trying to harm anyone, even when he was treated poorly by others. Yes, he threw a lot of tantrums, but that was only because of his inability to have his way, like a child. It struck me that only innocence makes life rich and not any amount of intellectual brilliance, material wealth, fame, and power. I wanted to be innocent like my father but was puzzled and confused. How does a clever person become innocent? I laughed as it looked like an oxymoron, but I was determined to figure it out, whatever it took.

Unlike my father, whom I considered weak, my mother, Rajeswari, was a strong woman. She always insisted on diligence and whole-hearted commitment to anything I did. She did not accept half measures. My mother, who did not attend school and was married as a child, raised a highly educated family of ten, with five of her children, including two daughters, gaining Ph.Ds. in mathematics, science or engineering. Yes, growing up, I was not materially well-off, but I could not have asked for better parents and siblings.

But, my early years at school were a disaster.

My elders told me that I was a precocious kid who often got into trouble. I was admitted to the third grade of an elementary school when I was only six-years-old. I was punished for being playful, which was mistaken for irreverence. When I became notorious for mischief, other kids invariably pointed fingers at me to escape punishment, even when they were the perpetrators. The teacher severely caned me without checking, even when I had done nothing wrong. I lost trust in the teacher, skipped school, and roamed the big city with vagabonds. A six-year-old kid!

The school was about five miles away from home and required a commute on the local train. I left home in the morning with other kids and returned in the evening with them, pretending to have been at school all the time. As I am separated from my closest siblings on either side by five years, no one else from the family went to the same school at that time. None was the wiser, until my annual progress report showed that I had to repeat the third grade for lack of attendance and performance. It did not bother me, as I did not know what it meant until I saw the sad face of my parents. When asked why I did not attend school, I told them the truth: I did not like getting beaten by the teacher for the mischief that I did not commit.

They put me in another school that was founded by Christian missionaries (The Society for the Propagation of Gospels (SPG)). It also required a similar commute. It was the best thing that happened in my young life. The class teacher, Williams-sir (that's how I remember him), never punished any kid; not even a harsh word. He was most affectionate and told amazing stories. He inspired me for the rest of my life. I consider myself extremely fortunate to have had such a wonderful teacher at that young age. But he was an exception. There were other teachers who slapped me so hard that their fingerprints would stay on my tender cheeks for a long time. After slapping me on one cheek, they invariably asked me to show my other cheek and slapped it too! What a convoluted way to practice Jesus's teachings!

I was then transferred to a school that was founded by a Muslim king (Mahbub), where my problems were less severe, although I continued to get caned all the way to the end of high school. I completed school with high honors and received the prestigious National Scholarship to pursue higher studies. I obtained a degree in mechanical engineering from Osmania University named after another Muslim king (Osman), and received a master's degree in aeronautics from the Indian Institute of Science that was founded by Tata, a Zoroastrian philanthropist.

I was selected to go to the Soviet Union on a faculty-exchange program. I spent over three years in the atheistic, communist Soviet Union, where I obtained Ph.D. degree from Moscow State University. I was a professor at IITB for over a decade before coming to the US to conduct research at NASA, which is located in the Bible Belt. Thus, I have been exposed to many religions and even communism, but I do not subscribe to any of them.

To be non-religious is not rare among Hindus. In fact, for millennia, atheism was viewed as a viable alternative to theism. The Buddha and Mahavir did not believe in God. In the epic poem *Bhagavad Gita*, Krishna, who is considered an avatar or god-incarnate by Hindus, identified himself with Kapila, a quintessential atheist and the author of atheistic Samkhya philosophy (Ballantyne 2001). Thus, as god himself revered an atheist, my non-religious nature did not cause an earthquake or tsunami at home.

What I realized on the tennis court was that my father's strength was emotional, not intellectual, although he had a liberal arts degree and held a mid-level management position. My father was an orthodox Hindu with a clean-shaven head but for small tufts of hair hanging at the rear of the head. His first name and my middle name, Margan, means a guide (on the spiritual path). *Marg* in Sanskrit means path. The Buddha's *Ashtanga Arya Marg* is translated as the eight-fold Noble Path. *Ashtanga* means eight limbs and *Arya* means noble.

My father loved classical south Indian music. He and my eldest sister were talented enough to be invited to perform on All India Radio, the only radio station at that time within a 200-mile radius. They used to practice long hours on Sundays. I used to sit near them and hear them sing. They let me play the harmonium to produce the monotone background sound. My father used to pray every day for over an hour and it was my duty to collect flowers from our small garden and from the neighborhood for his prayer.

My father was innocent, vulnerable, and playful like a child. His strength was not *thinking*, but *feeling*, which was my weakest cognitive function. I used to think that he was a loser, but ironically, I ended up being a big loser by my own standards. However, what I gained from the loss was beyond my wildest imagination as I tried to learn from my father.

After that incident on the tennis court, I wanted to write a loving letter to my father (he did not have a telephone and there was no internet at that time), stating how much I really admired him, and how much I wanted to be like him. I knew that he would be immensely happy to receive such a letter from me. In the past, even when I wrote harsh letters to him, he told others how well I expressed myself in English! He was proud of my command over the English language, as much as he was of his knowledge of Shakespeare. While others, including my mother, were upset by what they considered was my irreverent attitude, he allowed me to fearlessly express myself. He seemed to have realized that I innately cared for him.

As luck would have it, he passed away that very week before I could send him the letter. Strangely, according to my siblings who were with him during his last hours, he was wearing the wristwatch and shirt that I had presented to him during my previous visit to India. He was apparently remembering his prodigal son at the very end. I have never cried so much in my life.

I made a strange and irrevocable decision to be like him: innocent, vulnerable, playful, and emotionally contented. Winning and losing did not matter. I was still interested in research but let go of any desire for recognition from others. I saw no point in chasing a mirage.

As Charles Dickens observed in the *Tale of Two Cities*, it was the best of times, it was the worst of times; it was a time of despondency, and it was a time for action. I was already middle-aged, but as my mother always advised me, it was never too late for me to grow up. She admonished me with the same words even when I was sixty and told her that I was going to retire from work. She asked me when I was going to really start working! She was something.

I had to draw on all my inner strength to face reality with integrity. I began to explore my innate nature. I decided to become a passive observer to see how the mind handles situations even when I knew that others were trying to hurt me. I started observing with an open mind and let the scene unfold itself without trying to influence it. I began to see reality as it is without being perturbed by what others did. Until then, I knew a little about outer space exploration, but this was going to be an exploration of another kind: inner space, of the mind and emotions. And incomparably more exciting and challenging.

I love technical research. However, I am also keenly aware of the limitations of logic and reason. Having trained myself to be a hard-core intellectual, it was the significance of emotion that stunned me on the tennis court as I thought of my father. As I never had any desire for harming others, the problem reduced to finding ways not to get hurt by others, even without knowing or wanting to know what they were trying to do. It was challenging.

I started a company and named it Tao Systems, with *Balance in Technology* as its motto. When some of my Indian friends complained about why I chose a Chinese and not an Indian name, I started another company, Agora Enterprises, in memory of Socrates. I never heard from them again. Pete, a retired NASA director and Don, my former branch head, who had also retired, kindly helped me during the initial phase of the company. I also received guidance and support from Dave, a NASA legal counsel. I am grateful to all of them.

I began receiving funding from federal agencies for innovative research under the SBIR Program and collaborated with leading universities and research organizations in the U.S. and in Europe. We worked with major aircraft and submarine manufacturers and provided technical support for the winning sailboat teams that competed for the America's Cup (Screirer 2003). NASA highlighted our innovations in their Spinoffs and Tech Briefs

(NASA-TechBrief 2010), (NASA-Spinoff 2010), and (NASASpinoff 2019). Our innovations were highlighted in Aviation Week and Space Technology (AW&ST), the most widely read aerospace magazine.

In parallel, I began searching for the answers to my emotional problems, but I had no clue where to look. I was not sure if I would ever find it. I decided to explore my mind, conduct systematic experimentation, and let nature reveal the truth when the time was right, if ever.

In science, we conduct systematic research to reduce the complexity of the problem and eliminate known inconsistencies in the prevailing model. It may then only take a small trigger for a new paradigm to suddenly emerge. For instance, a falling apple triggered Newton to intuitively discover gravitation. Fortunately, I did not have to be brilliant like Newton, because my goal was not *a discovery of the unknown but a recovery of the known*, the key to my mental wellbeing.

I intuitively knew that *my feelings, thoughts, words, and actions must remain in harmony* for my mental wellbeing, as any discord among them caused mental disturbances. As it was also clear that I had little control over the large number of external variables, I decided to depend on the only variable that was known to me: myself. I realized that I must systematically reduce the complexity of the problem based on what is innately known to me, reject the unverifiable, and conduct experiments to eliminate internal contradictions.

I decided to explore my mind, even if it took the rest of my life. My children had completed their education and were independent. I made adequate financial arrangements for my wife who was in India taking care of her ailing father. I sought solitude.

I wrote to a Japanese Zen monastery in Sogenji for a possible stay. I conveyed that I was not religious and was not interested in questions regarding the purpose and meaning of life, etc. They were very welcoming. I was told that I would be at the bottom of the totem pole and had to obey the orders of everyone above me. I thought it was wonderful to have others look after me. An eleven-year-old Norwegian kid (Eljas) was my immediate boss! He was an awesome kid.

The monastery at Sogenji is located in Okayama prefecture. It is located in picturesque surroundings with hills and small ponds. There were residents from Australia, Canada, Europe, and the USA. I was given a tiny room in a small building on top of a hill. I was the only male in the building with eight rooms, one common bathroom, a toilet, and an exercise room. An Australian resident joked that I was the only rooster in the henhouse. The temple, meditation hall, kitchen, and other residential buildings were at the foot of the hill. We had a rough passage with unevenly spaced stones to walk down the hill. I once tripped in the dark and my head fell dangerously close to a big rock. It reminded me of my childhood.

There was a large prayer hall where we chanted every morning. The *zendo*, where we did *zazen*, could accommodate about sixty people, on three long platforms. Young male practitioners used the same platforms to sleep at night. There were small shelves above the platform where they kept their belongings, including the bedding. During my stay, there were about forty residents. All of us had to wear special robes. Casual dress was not allowed. Even in freezing cold winter, we were not allowed to wear turtleneck sweaters or any clothing to cover our neck and above. It was really hard for me during the autumn months when the freezing cold wind blew across the aisle where I was sitting with a large open window right behind me.

I spent a little over four months in the Zen monastery doing *zazen* for nearly eight to ten hours a day, which began with full-throated chanting for an hour in the morning, without knowing the meaning of a single word. In addition, I also did yard work and house cleaning every day. As a part of monastic life, we went out begging once a month. We chanted loudly as we went door-to-door begging. People treated us well and were generous with their offerings.

I had no access to books, newspapers, a telephone, a computer, internet, or a TV during my stay at the monastery. I rarely talked. It was most peaceful. My mind settled down and became a quiet observer. Trees were trees, hills were hills, birds were birds, fish were fish, and people were people. I was just one among them in a mysterious communion.

During meditation, a couple of monks or nuns patrolled the hall with a flat cane. They would respectfully stand in front of those who tended to doze off and give four blows on the shoulder blade to make them alert. It was a nightmare for me, as it reminded me of my childhood teachers, but thanks to Eljas, I escaped from getting hit even once. He used to alert me in a timely manner (when the cane-toting monk or nun entered our aisle). The only time I got hit was when the Zen Master Shodo Harada Roshi ceremoniously gave four blows to everyone without exception. And then he stopped hitting me, while he continued to hit all others, including some who were older than me. I wondered why he spared me, but being prudent, I did not ask him.

Life in the monastery was rigorous. The wakeup time was 3:30 a.m. Loud chanting in the prayer hall for an hour was followed by *zazen* for two hours. Following a light breakfast eaten in silence and in a ritual manner, we had to wash the dishes and return them to their shelves. It was followed by an hour for housecleaning. I had to scrub the floors, wash the windows, bathrooms and toilets. They teased me for my awkward way of cleaning and wondered aloud if I had ever done a day's hard work all my life.

It was followed by two hours of fieldwork; cleaning the yards, raking leaves, watering plants, cleaning the gutter, etc. until lunchtime. A ritualistic lunch was, followed by washing and drying the dishes and returning them to their shelves. Dining tables and benches were stashed away. Food was always healthy and of high quality. It was vegetarian, which was my only pre-requisite before I chose to go to the monastery. After lunch, I was allowed, with permission, to go to the town center for personal needs. Bicycles were available. The town was so safe that I could safely leave the bicycle unlocked at any place. Any packages left on the bicycle were also safe. It was a beautiful experience.

Supper was left-over food.

The day ended with another five to six hours of zazen followed by brief chanting. A couple of us were chosen to do ritual patrolling of all the buildings accompanied by loud chanting to make sure everything and everyone was safe before retiring to bed.

Two residents were selected every night for kitchen duty to prepare breakfast and lunch for all the next day. On one occasion, Eljas was the chef, and I was his assistant. He taught me how to make veggie pizza with corn and pineapple toppings. For a guy who has never cooked at home (growing up in a patriarchal society, my mother, my elder sisters, three elder sisters-in-law, and after marriage, my dear wife, never let me cook), cooking was a new experience and I seem to have done a good job. My *samosa* was a hit.

In addition to regular zazen, there were special Zen retreats (*sesshin*). Some even came from Europe for these retreats that lasted about a week with over twelve hours of meditation per day. It was intense. The day started as usual at 3:30 a.m. and ended around 11 p.m. There was no time even for taking a bath. There was a communal bath on the third day. I managed to wriggle permission to have a private bath every day. The rigorous retreats were meant to accelerate awakening (*satori*). I did three such retreats during my stay; but no *satori*.

The only time I heard from anyone from home was when my wife called the monastery to check on my wellbeing. We were strictly discouraged from talking to each other during work, *zazen*, chanting, and meals. I came across young people who had very troubled minds. I did not probe, but I could feel the deep need in them for mental peace. I noticed that some of them uncontrollably sobbed during *zazen*. It must have been cathartic. The atmosphere was energizing.

It was quiet, except for the songs and chirps of birds in the surrounding trees. For yard work, I had a favorite spot near the pond with cherry blossom trees. I would go there every morning to rake leaves and clean up the place. Colorful *koi* fish would come near the shore when I offered them food. It was the most peaceful and scenic spot in the monastery.

I met a tall, well-built, and middle-aged monk. He had a rough exterior, walking like a soldier with measured steps. He was a senior monk who often patrolled the *zendo* and delivered four lusty blows to awaken anyone tending to doze off. He was strict and to many, and especially to a Jewish practitioner, he seemed quite intimidating. When we got to know each other, he praised how alert I was, always sitting upright like a statue. He commented that my Indian background in yoga was probably why I was so good at meditation.

I assured him that it was not the case. "I was not meditating at all," I said, "but a nervous wreck trying to avoid blows from you!"

He roared with laughter when he heard that, and said he meant well. I agreed that he kept me awake and alert alright.

I inquired what had made him become a Buddhist monk. He said his parents were a part of Nazi Germany. He loathed that era in German history and found peace and fulfillment in Buddhism. While I admired his actions, I also told him that, as a human being, I was also responsible for what happened in Germany although I was not a German.

It was a mere accident that he was born to German parents and I was born to Indian parents. If I were born to German parents and grew up in Germany during the rule of Hitler, I might have done exactly what his parents did because I too would have been mentally conditioned like them. I was fortunate to have been born in India at the end of the colonial era and the ideas of Mahatma Gandhi were still fresh and vibrant. Mental conditioning brings about identification and clinging to a self-image, that of a German, Indian, Nigerian, Chinese, black, brown, white, etc. It is important to stop clinging to any image, however exalted or undesirable it might be.

He appeared relieved and happy to note that a complete stranger like me was able to empathize with him. We became close. When I left the monastery, he gave me a ride to the railway station to see me off, gave me a bear hug, and waited till the bullet train left the station. He was truly a gentle giant.

My Last Day at Sogenji

The normal day ended with about five hours of *zazen*. There was a break for about a couple of minutes every half hour to stretch our legs with silent circumambulation of the *zendo*. As I was not used to such rigor, my knees hurt a lot. At the end of *zazen* every evening, we used to have *sanzen* (a one-on-one meeting with the Zen master).

The Roshi invariably asked me only one question "Are you one with the universe?"

My invariable response was, "Yes, except for my knees that are jutting out of the universe in pain, due to sitting cross-legged for hours!"

He never smiled; I received only stern looks from him. My schoolteachers would have certainly caned me if I had answered like that.

On the eve of my departure, there was a huge party to celebrate Founder's Day. Monks and nuns had come from various parts of Japan. *Sake* (rice wine) was flowing.

The Roshi kindly invited me for tea with him on the day of my departure. For the first time ever, on my request, he permitted me to ask him a couple of questions.

I said that I noticed that a lot of *sake* was consumed the previous day by the monks. I asked him, "When the monks were drunk with *sake*, did they see one or two universes? If they saw two, how did they become one with two universes?"

There was slight consternation on his face before he laughed loudly and said, "Neither one nor two. They were just happily drunk!"

I came back to the US laughing, happy that I did not get four blows with his ever-ready cane and glad that my playful nature had not abandoned me.

The End of My Search

My sojourn at the monastery resolved my internal contradictions and restored my joyful, playful, and creative nature, with no fear of ever losing them. I began to see reality as it was (and is) without projecting my values on it. I was content and happy to let my innate nature guide me.

I searched for the key to happiness in my head, but I found it in my heart.

Jesus offered a keyless entry with, "Knock, and it shall be opened to you." Poet Rabindranath Tagore, a Nobel Laureate, gave it a delightful twist when he observed (Tagore 1919), "Those who *want to love*, knock on the door; those who *are in love*, find the door open!" They were referring to the door to the heart.

The mind is usually filled with fear, anxiety, and insecurity, whereas the heart that is filled with love is naturally free and fearless. For millennia, theologians and intellectuals have been using belief system, logic, and reason to find the key through knowledge and information, but the *key to happiness is in the heart*.

Sitting quietly for hours on end with a blank mind and no concern for the future and chanting loudly for over an hour every day even without knowing what the words meant gave my mind a complete rest. It was like sleeping and yet being alert. It was mesmerizing to realize that the *self-image is like a shadow. It moves when the mind moves and stops when the mind stops. It does not have a separate existence.* We do not have to decorate it or struggle for its survival.

Mental disturbances naturally vanish when the mind ceases to move with external objects, including people. We are socially conditioned to cling to family, friends, relatives, race, tribe, organization, nation, etc. Self-image includes all their images. When we perceive harm to one set of images that we like, the *other set*, which we dislike, fights back. *Mental suffering is caused by clinging, comparing, and coveting between two sets of images within the same mind.*

It is not possible to willfully let go of clinging to self-image. However, we can voluntarily cease to harm *others*, i.e., fulfill the first principle: *"Do not do to others what you would not want others to do to you."* It opens the door to empathy and compassion when we realize that the image of the other is also within us.

Thanks to my parents, teachers, and my innate temperament, I naturally fulfilled the first principle. It was the second principle that initially posed problems. I could not *"Maintain feelings, thoughts, words, and actions in har-*

mony." Intense *zazen* practice at Sogenji, and persistent question from the Roshi asking me whether "I was one with the universe," made it clear that my only obstacle was not my knees, but my self-image that set it apart from *others*.

Feelings, thoughts, words, and actions naturally remain in harmony with the realization that the self and the other are the same; they are *not two*. The Vedic Rishis were right, after all, when they propounded the advaita (not-two) philosophy (Easwaran 2007).

I started out in search of myself and found *no-self*. It was, quite literally, *much ado about no-thing*. When there is *no-self*, there is no button to trigger emotions. The door remains open but there is *no-thing* inside! No effort is needed to balance reason, emotion and action. There is *no-thing* to balance!

A huge burden was lifted off my back. For good. Being myself as nature created was the naked truth. No wonder Jesus said, "When you lose everything, you gain everything!"

3

The Four Paths

When you come to a fork on the road, take it!
—Yogi Berra

Sensing, feeling, thinking, and intuition are four cognitive functions that we use to perceive, judge, and respond to reality (Berens 1999). Although the skill-level may vary, sensing, thinking, and feeling are common to the entire animal kingdom. We judge and respond to reality with feelings that are rooted in emotion, the driving force of life, and intuition that is logically inexplicable. Animals excel in sensing, but human beings have developed thinking and intuition far beyond the known animal world.

Primitive societies valued physical strength (*sensing*) to deal with predators and enemies. It led to tremendous progress in agriculture, building construction, weaponry, and various activities that required physical strength. With the advance of science and technology, the emphasis shifted to the intellect (*thinking*). Today, people tend to gravitate toward the acquisition of knowledge and information in search of greater opportunities. *Feeling* remains one of the least valued functions, as it seems to offer little material benefit.

Evolutionary forces, genetics, and environmental conditions have made one of the functions, viz., *sensing, feeling, or thinking,* stronger than the others in an individual. In other words, two of them are relatively weak compared to the dominant one. If we look at them as the three legs of a tripod, thinking has become much longer than sensing, while feeling remains stunted. A tripod is unstable when its legs are of different lengths, regardless of how strong or long one leg is.

Mental harmony and freedom require that these three cognitive functions are balanced.

They may be most skewed today, but differences have always been present in people from ancient times. The problem and its solution were apparently known to the ancients. In *Bhagavad Gita* (Fosse 2007), the poet Vyasa described four distinct paths to liberation. Each path is tailor-made for individuals with one of the four functions as their dominant cognitive function, but with the objective of realizing balance among them.

Krishna at Kurukshetra

Sage Vyasa chose the eve of a brutal war on the battlefield of Kurukshetra that witnessed the slaughter of hundreds of thousands of armed men over a feud between warring cousins as the setting for describing his insights. Like the Civil War in the USA, the warring factions included friends, relatives, teachers, loved ones as well as sworn enemies fighting against each other. The poet used it presumably to depict the struggle waged in every mind. He conveyed the message through Krishna, a remarkable king who opted not to fight, transferred his hundred-thousand strong army to fight on behalf of the enemies, vowed not use any weapon, voluntarily disarmed himself, and became a charioteer for the prince Arjuna.

Krishna walked free amidst enemies and mayhem. Elders worshiped him while even his enemies sought his advice and preferred to die in his hands. It was on this battlefield that Krishna expounded four paths to liberation, which had a profound impact on great thinkers like Emerson and Thoreau, and influenced the entire spectrum of people, from war hawks to pacifists like Mahatma Gandhi. A king himself, but unarmed, unperturbed, and serene, Krishna cleared the doubts experienced by the prince Arjuna on the eve of the eighteen-day bloodbath.

I sought Krishna himself to describe his four paths to liberation.

Significance of Innate Nature (*Swadharma*)

"In the *Bhagavad Gita*, your advice to Arjuna was to remain steadfast in following his innate nature (*swadharma*). What is your innate nature?"

Krishna said. "Playfulness is my innate nature and so is yours. Children are playful. Animals are playful. Nature is playful. You play according to her rules (inviolable laws). Nature is infinitely curious, creative, and playful, like a child. She has all the resources at her disposal, but like Dennis the Menace, she is still looking for something to find. You do not have to be an avatar, a prophet, a messiah, or a rocket scientist to participate in her adventure however brief your sojourn. *Being true to your innate nature (swadharma) is all that she expects from you.*

"Hindus and Muslims look at each other with suspicion and animosity but Muhammad and I were quite alike. He too did not seek wars but bravely fought the wars that were imposed on him. He was essentially a peaceful businessman. He too had implicit trust in his innate nature.

"You have the option to live to your fullest potential by being playful and creative, treating everyone as a friend, or be greedy, deceitful, and cowardly like the insecure rulers who suppress people with repressive laws. They spread suffering among people who cannot effectively respond to treachery and deception that are supported by a vast army. Muhammad and I dealt with them using the only language they understood."

"I see ugliness in human relationships," I observed. "Terrorism, racism, and suppression of human rights are rampant. I am caught between various emotions: war or peace, passive non-violence or active involvement, forest or society? How do I reconcile these varied emotions? Life seems so short."

"Yes, life is short," agreed Krishna, "but it is also like a playground. You get one opportunity to play the game. When you play the game according to your innate nature, nature makes you happy. Being aligned with her is enough. The word loser does not exist in her vocabulary.

"Nature has given you a simple monitor: *you suffer when your actions are not aligned with your innate nature (swadharma). It is the key that you could use to monitor your thoughts, feelings, and words until your actions are completely in tune with your innate nature.*

"The tool that nature has given you to realize this goal is emotion. Watch your emotion carefully with sensitivity. It would reveal the trajectory of the mind and the state of mental health. *Any mental disturbance or internal discord is a clear indication that your mind is deviating from your innate nature by clinging to an external source and moving with it.* It suggests that you need to take corrective steps and return to your innate nature."

Krishna continued. "Emotion is life whereas reason is a sophisticated tool for the mind to use. Human beings are not robots. You are able to logically model the physical world, but you have hardly scratched the surface with regard to emotions (Adolphs 2018). Their origin and purpose remain a mystery. They are as mysterious as life itself.

"Your quest for the arts, music, sports, science, exploration, fighting, peace, friendship, love, hatred, etc. are all based on emotion. Reasons are an after-thought to explain or justify your response. Undaunted by known risks, brave pioneers are willing to go on a voyage to Mars. At the other extreme, there are suicide bombers who blow themselves apart and kill others in the process. Nature creates emotions that cannot be satisfactorily explained with the intellect.

"I asked Arjuna to follow his innate nature. I did not threaten him with adverse consequences if he did not follow my advice. I told him that he would suffer if he acted against *his* innate nature. There were no ifs and buts. Your actions must flow naturally from your inmost core. Arjuna was free to do what he deemed fit.

"*When you are in tune with your innate nature, your actions will be harmonious. When you are aligned with your innate nature, reason and emotion will function harmoniously like the two wings of a bird. Align yourself with your innate nature.*

"I shall describe each path now."

1. The Path of Action (*Karma Yoga*)

"For people whose dominant cognitive function is *sensing*, I suggested *karma yoga* or the path of action without selfish motives. Unconditional. No *quid pro quo*. Karma literally means action. All living beings are continuously involved in action that is dictated by the need for biological survival and physical well-being. Commitment to action would naturally bring out other faculties that remain relatively dormant within you.

"Playfulness is an inherent quality of people whose dominant cognitive function is sensing. They naturally gravitate toward efforts that require physical action. They excel in sports and other action-oriented endeavors. However, in a society that is driven by productivity and wealth, one's purpose is usually defined by the powerful. The *sensors* often feel lost in such a world, as energy is dissipated in wars and conflicts.

"Karma yoga asks the individual to diligently pursue actions that come naturally. There may be a tendency to thoughtlessly tread on others without compunction. Hence, follow the first principle: "*Do not do to others what you would not want them to do to you.*" A conscious effort to refrain from harming others will reveal the need for empathy and to be thoughtful. The path of karma yoga would naturally compel you to strengthen the feeling and thinking functions. Once all these three functions are balanced, intuition will naturally take over.

"*Muhammad created an effective path for those with* sensing *as their dominant cognitive function, with emphasis on mercy, compassion, and universal camaraderie (brotherhood).* Muhammad's life itself is a beautiful example of how an ordinary merchant became an action-oriented thinker, a warrior, and a compassionate individual.

Charitable work, Doctors without Borders, Habitat for Humanity, People for Ethical Treatment of Animals, etc. are carried out by dedicated *karma yogis* who find their work emotionally fulfilling."

2. The Path of Devotion (*Bhakti Yoga*)

"Jesus introduced the *bhakti yoga* or the path of devotion for those who respond to reality primarily through *feeling*. A large segment of the human population is driven by feelings. It includes almost half the population, women, who are naturally motivated by feelings of love and caring and endowed with qualities that promote the creation and nurture of life.

"An individual with feeling as the dominant cognitive function is naturally compassionate, caring, and kind toward other beings. However, adversarial social orders tend to exploit such people as they are viewed as vulnerable and weak. Even Nietzsche thought that the people of the East were weak and timid. Voltaire observed that Indians were too weak to either harm others or even to protect themselves. Feelers are prone to being exploited if they follow their natural instincts with weak peripheral functions. Many become conditioned to protect themselves from being exploited through clever means or become submissive.

"*Jesus advised such people to boldly and honestly practice their innate nature.* He offered no compromise. His objective was not to create a martyr or a scapegoat for others to exploit but to let the innate intelligence of these people come to the fore and protect them from exploitation. He fully knew that the *thinking* and *sensing* functions of these people would be strengthened when they boldly meet the challenges they encounter in the society in response to their innate kindness and empathy. When *sensing, feeling,* and *thinking* are balanced, intuition will naturally take over and reveal the truth that liberates.

"The important point to keep in mind is that one has to remain alert and constantly strive to strengthen the perceived weak areas until dynamic mental balance is achieved. When innate feeling is diligently pursued with courage, individuals will naturally gain the intellectual power, and the required physical and material resources to lead a loving, generous, and compassionate life without being hurt in the process. It requires commitment and diligent practice, and nature will provide the required internal energy and mental resources to attain it.

"As Jesus aptly put it, 'Knock and it shall be given.'

"*Bhakti Yoga* is the fastest path to liberation. However, as it is also the riskiest path, only the truly courageous people with childlike innocence are able to follow it. It will result in people like Mother Teresa and Martin Luther King, Jr. People who work for the prevention of cruelty to animals and to lift people from poverty belong to this group."

3. The Path of Wisdom (*Jnana Yoga*)

"The path of wisdom is primarily meant for those who depend on *thinking* to perceive and respond to reality. It might apply to scientists, philosophers, and the like. A logically verifiable reason for the existence of the universe or life does not exist. Creation is a mystery. There is nothing your intellect can do about it except wonder in awe and try to understand its laws.

"*Jnana yoga* or the path of wisdom takes you to the edge of your intellectual prowess to reveal the limitations of logic and reason. When you gain the required courage to cross the intellectual boundaries, you will be awakened to the true nature of emotions that, like Nietzsche, you too may have ignored as a weakness. *When you are awakened, you'd continue to have your great intellect, but nature will use your intellect appropriately.*

"*The Buddha devised ingenious ways to strengthen the weaker aspects of intellectuals, which are generally feeling and sensing.* He accomplished it by creating a sangha where he encouraged the disciples to become mendicants. It made them lose their conceit and become humble. Secondly, it allowed them to recognize first-hand, how kind people were in feeding them and providing alms without expecting anything in return. Even poor people shared whatever little they could afford. It gradually introduced qualities of compassion and empathy in his disciples. The need to build their own living quarters and take care of the sangha made them physically strong. Martial arts, including archery, Kung Fu, etc., were also practiced by the disciples.

"Thus, the Buddha created the environment for cognitive balance to occur naturally. The path of jnana yoga takes considerable time to realize dynamic mental balance because intellectuals tend to cling to their much-vaunted intellect that has high social value.

Mahatma Gandhi and Nelson Mandela were intellectuals who became compassionate and non-violent freedom fighters."

4. The Royal Path (*Raja Yoga*)

"*Patanjali systematized Raja yoga or the Royal Path for those who are gifted with intuition.* Such people generally would like to find the answers themselves without teachings or dependence on external authority. Patanjali's *Ashtanga Yoga Sutra* is a systematic approach that focuses on integrating body, mind, and emotion. His integral approach is amenable to rational exploration.

"Patanjali does not offer any teachings to bridge the gap between meditation and samadhi (balance and harmony). He leaves it to the individual's intuition. Patanjali is most helpful to those who do not need his help! People who practice Raja yoga are quiet and independent."

"**In summary**, it makes no difference which path you take. The goal is the same: the realization of your innate nature (*swadharma*). Be true to yourself. Do not copy others however exalted, famous, or venerated they might be. Nature has created a unique role-model for you: you. Being true to your innate nature will naturally ensure mental balance, harmony, and freedom. You have strayed far from your innate nature because of social pressures and incentives. *You are not the image that society has made you believe. You are what nature has created: a unique and mysterious individual. Remain true to it.*"

The Language of Nature

Nature speaks a silent language.
Her word is the Law.

Whether God exists or not is a moot point, but it is indubitable that a silent, invisible, immutable, and inviolable law (or a set of laws) of nature governs the universe. The law may be silent and invisible, but its effects are usually loud and clear. A cat may not have heard of Newton, but it instinctively avoids a precipitous fall. *Awareness of the laws of nature and living in accordance with them is the key to our freedom and wellbeing.*

Religion and science trace the origin of the laws of nature to the beginning of creation and the Big Bang, respectively. The Bible asserted, "In the beginning was the Word." The Buddha referred to the law as *dhamma*. It was the Tao for Laozi and *sanatana dharma* or the eternal principle of Vedic Rishis, who also observed that truth is one and the wise call it by different names (*ekam sat vipra bahuda vadanti*). *Davar, dhamma, dharma,* logos, the Tao, truth, and the word are different names for the law. Their view of creation is practically identical with the modern view of the cosmos as described in the next section.

Science & Religion

The cosmos consists of the unmanifest (zero or emptiness) and the manifest (creation). An invisible, invariant, and inviolable law (or a set of laws) governs the dynamical changes that take place in creation. Emptiness, dynamically changing creation, and the law are the three aspects of nature. There is no more and no less.

Scientists have developed models to describe dynamic changes that occur in the cosmos. They discovered laws of nature that drive these changes with positive and negative forces (Fig. 4.1a). For example, forces of attraction (positive, creation) and repulsion (negative, destruction) characterize gravitation, electromagnetism, nuclear power, etc. They are symbolic and do not carry human values like good and evil, right and wrong, love and hatred, etc.

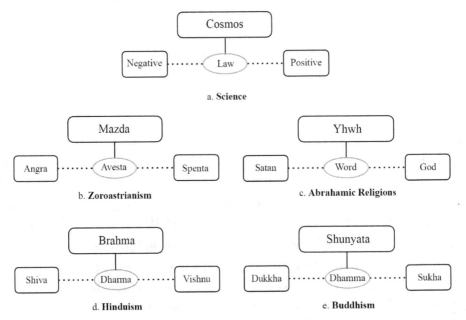

Figure 4.1. **Trinity in Science and Religions.**

Let us briefly examine how the scientific model compares with Zoroastrianism, Abrahamic religions, Hinduism, and Buddhism (Fig. 4.1b-e).

Zarathustra was, perhaps, the first to express the nature of reality (Fig. 4.1b) in a symbolic manner (Kapadia 1905). He referred to the origin of creation as *Ahura Mazda*; *Spenta mainyu* (good mind) *and Angra mainyu* (evil mind) as the positive and negative forces that effect changes in accordance with the laws that he described in *Zend Avesta*. Awareness of the law allows us to realize what is good (creative) and what is evil (destructive). His perception is in agreement with science, except that the positive and negative forces were expressed in terms of perceived human values of good and evil.

Abraham looked at the *unmanifest* origin of creation as Yhwh (Fig. 4.1c). Obviously, none preceded Yhwh, as zero or emptiness is the origin and there is no god before it. He referred to the law that governed creation as davar. Muhammad also observed that there was no god, but only Allah. The cosmos is governed by Allah. They looked at the positive and negative forces in terms of human values of good (God or angel) and evil (Satan or devil). Abrahamic religions also agree with the scientific model of the cosmos. As in science, the focus is on realizing the nature of the law (davar, logos, or word) or Allah.

Hinduism describes reality (Fig. 4.1d) in terms of Brahma, Vishnu, and Shiva. They called it *trimurti or three faces of reality*. They depict the same ideas of Zarathustra. Mazda was replaced by Brahma, *Spenta Mainyu* by Vishnu (Preserver), and *Angra Mainyu* by Shiva (Destroyer). Hindus reversed the roles of Spenta Mainyu and Angra Mainyu as Vishnu, also known as *Angara*, is a positive force. Hinduism also focuses on becoming aware of the eternal law (*sanatana dharma*) and living in accordance with it to realize liberation (*moksha*).

The Buddha looked at the unmanifest (Shunyata, zero or emptiness) as the substratum on which creation exists. (Fig. 4.1e) Thereby, he eliminated the need for God as a creator. He looked at creation as a dynamic system that is continuously changing in accordance with the law (dhamma). He referred to the impermanent nature of creation as *anitta* (transient).

Instead of calling them positive and negative forces that are based on our value system (a coordinate system), the Buddha referred to them in terms of what is innately known to everyone as *Sukha* (contentment) and *Dukkha* (discontent). He observed that positive (*Sukha*) and negative (*Dukkha*) forces naturally cancel each other at the center (for an *anatta* or no-self). According to the Buddha, we experience *nirvana* when we are centered, as everything gets done by nature and we become a pure observer. The Buddha's approach was *coordinate-free*.

Both science and religions assert the following:

1. Nature is governed by an invariant and inviolable law (or a set of laws).
2. Changes that occur in nature are either positive or negative in relation to the chosen frame of reference (the coordinate frame).

If we are aware of the nature of the law, then we can live in accordance with it to ensure that the outcome is positive for our emotional (mental) wellbeing.

Thus, instead of placating mythical beings and clinging to outcomes with fear, anxiety and uncertainty, all we need to do is focus our efforts on becoming aware of the law that governs our lives and live in accordance with it. The *Buddha aptly called it Dhammapada, which literally means* "dhamma-path" or "*the law-path.*"

Freedom and the laws that impose constraints on freedom are complementary and not mutually antagonistic. In the absence of the laws that govern gravitation, nuclear forces, thermodynamics, electromagnetism, etc., there would be no atom, no molecule, no matter, no earth, no star, no galaxy, no universe, and certainly, no you, and no me! From giant galaxies to tiny atoms and from gigantic mammals to microorganisms, the integrity of a system depends on how various forces are dynamically balanced in accordance with the laws of nature that govern them. Our wellbeing depends on a delicate balance of various parameters.

The Importance of Balance

Zero and balance play a fundamental role in science, mathematics, and life. We obtain a correct solution when both sides of an equation are exactly balanced. Any residue that is different from zero is an error. The Buddha described nirvana as *samma-samadhi* or complete balance. *Samadhi* or balance was also the aim of Patanjali's *Ashtanga Yoga Sutra*. They were referring to mental balance with zero wasteful energy dissipation.

After watching the staggering drunk struggling in vain to insert his key to open the apartment door, a friendly neighbor offered to help. The drunk gracefully declined the offer saying, "I am doing just fine, thank you," but added on second thought, "I'd myself be able to insert the key if you could kindly hold the building from swaying."

Quite logical even in his inebriated state! Dysfunctional sensory-motor functions in an inebriated person adversely affect both physical balance and mental poise. A dualistic mind also exhibits similar characteristics with one major difference. A drunk sees a pair of blurred images of one objective reality, whereas a dualistic mind perceives polar opposite values such as good and evil, friend and foe, etc. of one subjective reality. The life of a dualistic mind is an unsteady maneuver between these two polar opposites. False perceptions of reality lead to a mental imbalance that could result in emotional disturbances, a metaphorical fall, and suffering.

We encounter imbalance at three levels. At the gross level, physical imbalance causes injury and pain. *Physiological imbalance* causes illness and pain. Its subtle source, e.g., pathogens, is invisible to our sense organs, but scientific tools are used to detect them. *Psychological or mental imbalance* causes mental disturbances in the form of fear, anxiety, insecurity, etc. It is abstract and invisible to both sensory organs and scientific tools.

Being blind, ignorant or unprepared to maintain the required balance could lead to instability with unintended consequences. For example, the Titanic struck an iceberg, became unstable, and sank in the Atlantic Ocean, killing over 1,500 people (Wincour 1960). Accretion of ice crystals on the airspeed probe of Air France Flight 447 resulted in its malfunction, which eventually led the aircraft to stall and crash into the Atlantic Ocean, killing all aboard (AirFrance 2012). My car hit an icy patch, skidded, crashed against a tree, and was totaled. The common cause for the above accidents, involving three vastly different transport systems was their inability to maintain the required balance for the intended trajectory.

A century ago, Emmy Noether (Brewer 1981) made a vital contribution to Einstein's theory of relativity when she showed that symmetry is the basis for conservation laws in physics. We instinctively maintain physical balance by controlling equal and opposite forces in accordance with Newton's third law. Symmetry and balance go together. Nature has designed both our sensory systems and mind to quickly detect any asymmetry. It allows us to recognize the source of imbalance and take corrective steps.

Our mind-body unit is a dynamic system that consumes, stores, and expends energy. We experience sound physical health when food intake is used to meet the normal physiological needs of the body. We practice hygiene, eat a balanced diet, and do physical exercise to maintain physiological balance and enjoy robust physical health. When we are healthy, we may feel as if we could climb Mt. Everest barefoot. On the other hand, we may find it difficult to even walk to the bathroom when we experience debilitating pain caused by illness due to an imbalance in the physiological system. In this case, a part of the energy (food) is diverted away from normal requirements to fight organisms that cause illness, resulting in energy dissipation that is experienced as pain. It is used by doctors for diagnosis and medical treatment.

Similarly, mental suffering occurs when energy is diverted to fight extraneous feelings, thoughts, words, and actions that are associated with emotional imbalance. The most effective approach to realize emotional balance is by maintaining zero energy dissipation on mental disturbances. It depends on knowing the nature of the self.

Nature of the Self

When I was a kid, my grandfather, who was a professor of mathematics, teased me with the question, "What is India's greatest contribution to mathematics?" Seeing a blank expression on my face, he answered, "Nothing, a big zero!" And laughed.

Actually, the concept of zero may have originated from religion and not mathematics. Zero is merely a symbol for non-existence. Zero is uncreated, omnipresent, invisible, and indestructible, qualities that mimic the conventional concept of God. Ironically, atheists reject God, presumably because there is no evidence for God's existence, but in science and mathematics, they use zero that, by definition, does not exist!

Zero could be used for *Debugging the Mind* just as zero is used to solve problems in science.

The Buddha did just that.

For instance, the Buddha made prolific use of the words shunya and shunyata. In *Sanskrit*, shunya means zero, and shunyata means nothingness or emptiness that is unmanifest to the sensory organs. He observed that the *dhamma* or the law that governs life is unmanifest (*sarva dharma shunyata*) and that there is no-self (anatta).

The self is a great mystery. It is so close and yet so far. No one has seen it, nobody seems to know whence it emerged at birth and where it is headed, if anywhere, at death. We do not even know what happens to it every night when we are asleep. According to the Buddha, there is no-self, and our perceptions of the self are illusory. In sharp contrast, we have a strong sense of self and believe that it is real. How do we know that the Buddha himself was not deluded? He simply announced that he had become "awakened." We too become awakened every morning, but he probably did not mean that either. Do we trust him or our actual experiences?

The Buddha was awakened to a state of no-mind, which he referred to as nirvana. He did not or could not logically explain how he realized nirvana or no-self (anatta). According to Buddhist texts, his internal contradictions were at a boiling point, but they suddenly vanished, like a dream or nightmare disappears on waking up. It was like getting rid of a debilitating disease after a long-drawn struggle. It was like a child who suddenly realized dynamic physical balance and learned to ride a bicycle without the fear of falling.

Views on the nature of the self vary, from the Vedic Rishis who identified themselves with the creator (*Aham Brahmasmi*) (Madhavananda 2015) to the Buddha's observation of its non-existence (anatta). Some religions believe that the self or the soul is headed for heaven or eternal hell. Others like Hinduism and Buddhism believe in reincarnation. Our present life, according to them, is the result of our actions (karma) in past lives. When I asked a famous Hindu Swami, what caused my action in my very first life, he turned to the next questioner.

Be that as it may, the self-image is a persistent phenomenon that does not disappear except when we are in deep sleep, unconscious, or under anesthesia. In fact, it may not be a stretch of the imagination to state that our entire life seems to be built with and around images of how we define ourselves and others, but they have a bearing on our feelings, thoughts, words, and actions. Unlike the body that gets hurt only with direct physical contact, the "self" feels hurt, insulted, flattered, or elated even with words that are spoken or printed about it in a far-off place. The contact takes place at an abstract level.

We are constantly told to get rid of the ego. Such advice may be well-intentioned but futile because it is impossible to get rid of the ego. The ego is coupled to us like our shadow, which is long at sunrise and short at noon. Similarly, the ego or self-image is boosted by some and diminished by others, by the external light focused on it, but the real self remains invariant.

The easiest way to realize the nature of self-image is by conducting a thought experiment. Imagine that you are the only living being in the entire universe, with no one to insult or flatter you; no one to deceive or harm you. No one is competing with you for a job, no one is cutting you off on the highway, and no one is stealing anything from you. In such a scenario, self-image has no meaning or value; there is no one superior or inferior; there is no good or evil. It becomes clear that the idea of ego or self-image arises only with the presence of others.

There is nothing right or wrong about the ego or self-image. It is as natural as a shadow or reflection of our body. And as unreal. Clinging to the self-image is a tacit admission of dependence on others. Letting others determine our self-worth and struggling all our lives to make it look good is futile. It is best to let go of clinging to this image and be free. Self-image will automatically vanish when we are aware of our innate nature. Realizing our innate nature or the true nature of the self is critical for our mental wellbeing.

How to realize our innate nature by *Debugging the Mind* is described in Part II of the book.

The Self and Reality

The Buddha used the analogy of a wheel (*chakra*) to describe the relationship between the self and reality. He said that the self, like the center, has no dimension, physical attribute, or value. It does not have a physical existence. The center is the invariant frame of reference for the wheel. Points on the rim, on the other hand, have values (positive or negative in relation to the center). As the wheel turns, points on the rim follow a cyclic motion, sequentially moving forward, down, back, and finally up in every cycle but the center is stationary with no value.

When the mind clings to the periphery, it experiences emotions that continuously change; sometimes feeling elated (up or positive), sometimes depressed (down or negative), sometimes making progress (moving forward), and set back at other times. They define the trajectory of the mind. A point on the periphery constantly changes (good-evil, up-down, right-wrong, positive-negative, left-right, north-south, east-west, etc.) as the wheel rotates. In stark contrast, the center remains in dynamic balance, even as the wheel rotates. Values disappear at the center. Anatta (no-self) is the nature of the self at the center where the opposites are in perfect balance, where all contradictions disappear. There is no energy dissipation at the center. *The center that was never created and can never be destroyed, is invariant. Only the periphery undergoes changes.*

When we cling to the periphery or self-image, we hope to go up when we hit the bottom. When we are on top of the world, we are afraid of going down, which occurs inevitably as whatever brought us to the top wanes with time. Sometimes we feel like we have taken a few backward steps. All these changes mimic the behavior of a wheel in motion. Clinging to the image, the mind goes through endless cycles of progress and setback, depression and elation. Uncertainty causes fear, anxiety, and insecurity, which, in turn, cause energy dissipation.

In all these ups and downs, progress and regression, the center experiences an amazing stillness and serenity. The center (self) effortlessly goes wherever the wheel (nature) takes it. The non-moving and non-existing center effortlessly covers the same distance as the huffing and puffing rim. When we realize our innate nature, when we live in a state of letting go, nature takes us effortlessly to unexpected destinations in a wondrous manner. It is the *wu-wei* or action without action of Laozi.

We may think that we have made all the effort to get where we are but actually, nature has brought us where we are. Nature is responsible for our very existence but somewhere along the line, we became clever enough to think that we make things happen. How amusingly conceited! When Jesus said, "Thy will be done," he meant that the wheel takes you where it will. Life becomes an amazing adventure. We simply enjoy the free ride, without the vain struggle.

When we are centered, we do not use our minds; nature uses our minds. When centered, the mind is ecstatic, whereas it is eccentric when off-center. Emotions that emerge from the center are innate, direct from nature. The center is where contradictions vanish without a trace, and with complete obliteration of the opposites. It has no image.

Human interactions occur at the periphery between different spatial and temporal trajectories and values (perspectives of the past and the future, right and wrong, good and evil, etc.) of the participants. As conflicts and violent clashes of the random trajectories are inevitable at the periphery, people tend to seek security inside a fortified box, where they feel somewhat protected from perceived threats but live in constant fear, anxiety, and insecurity. They teach their children to live likewise and further reinforce the boxes by organizing people into a collective with similar fears and insecurities. These boxes are labeled religion, race, caste, family, tribe, nation, etc., that includes perceived friends and excludes perceived enemies.

It is interesting to compare the Buddha's chakra analogy with the Christian mystic, Meister Eckhart's description of God (the words in italics are mine) (Davis 1994): "God is infinite in his simplicity (*zero*) and simple (*zero*) in his infinity. Therefore, he is everywhere, and is everywhere complete. He is everywhere on account of his infinity and is everywhere complete on account of his simplicity. Only God flows into all things, their very essences. Nothing else flows into something else. God is in the innermost part of each and everything, only in its innermost part (*center*). To be full of things (*self-images*) is to be empty of God. To be empty of things (self-images) is to be full of God."

Although zero and infinity are used in mathematical and scientific research, no one, absolutely no one, including the most diehard atheist, has ever seen or measured them. However, they are useful concepts, the bedrock of modern mathematics, the purest form of logic known to us. The world has witnessed remarkable progress using zero in science and mathematics. Similar progress is possible toward the creation of a peaceful, joyful, and creative world if every individual becomes centered and realizes another type of zero: the true nature of the self.

Being Centered

The self, according to the Buddha, is devoid of physical attributes. Like the center of gravity, which is a point about which the mass is balanced in a gravitational field, the self is the center about which the mind is balanced in a field of consciousness. None of these concepts, viz., self, mind, center of gravity, consciousness and gravitation is manifest to our sense organs.

One of the strangest paradoxes in existence is the unmanifest or emptiness (null set) about which we know absolutely nothing, except that it exists. To know whether non-existence exists, we have to first define the meaning of existence itself. By definition, darkness, silence, and space denote the absence of light, sound, and matter respectively. We can't have music without silence. However, does silence exist? Was it created? We recognize the presence of light but what is darkness other than the absence of light? Was darkness created? Space is the absence of matter. Was space created? The manifest and the unmanifest dance together. One cannot exist without the other. In other words, existence is meaningless without the unmanifest. Non-existence (zero) is the invariant substratum on which we perceive the dynamics of existence.

The manifest physical world is in flux, dynamically transforming from one state to another, but darkness, silence, and space have neither a beginning nor an end in space or time. They are absolute and invariant, neither static nor dynamic. The idea of the creator of darkness, silence, and space makes no sense. Why do we clamor only for the creator of that which is manifest? How about the creator of the unmanifest? The physical world appears fragile as it morphs from one state to another whereas the unmanifest is indestructible, eternal, and immutable. Everything appears and disappears on this invariant unmanifest or vast emptiness. The unmanifest is infinitely vast compared to the manifest universe. So, the non-creator of the unmanifest is also infinitely more powerful than the creator of the manifest. Perhaps, the unmanifest is God, while the manifest is the devil's workshop!

Does nothing or zero exist? In a conventional sense, it does not exist, but we are intuitively cognizant of its non-existence in an abstract sense. I am not offended if someone tells me that zero does not exist although every aspect of my scientific research depends on it. It is not blasphemous to deny the existence of zero. Zero exists only as an abstract concept. It is the origin or absolute frame of reference for our number system and it also separates the positive from the negative. We seem to have total faith in *nothing*! The unmanifest is the god of religions.

It is in this sense that the self does not exist. When the Buddha observed that there is no-self, he did not mean that there is *no* self, but that there *is* no-self. The concept itself, obviously, does not end suffering, just as zero does not solve mathematical problems. We need to apply effective techniques to find the unique and non-trivial roots of the equation to solve the problem. Similarly, we need to find the roots of our mental problems through practical experimentation.

We encounter two types of challenges in life: central and peripheral. The central challenges in life are the existential issues, and the peripheral ones are the secondary ones. The existential issues are unique and absolute. It may be as simple as hunger and thirst, or more complex like freedom. The central issues are not subject to logic, reason, interpretation, judgment, or negotiation. They demand total responses.

It is possible to pretend to believe in and owe allegiance to an external authority such as a priest, prophet, king, flag, or even god, but in reality, the individual is the only, final and absolute authority when it concerns central issues. In fact, central issues correspond to an existential need that demands a total response and not an imaginary or speculative answer. People breathe, eat, and quench thirst without reading scriptures or listening to any sermons. Our central, existential needs are vital to our lives, which are met only at our center, within us. They are not negotiable.

The infinite existence or reality meets us at our center, the self. The beauty of the center is that it is able to accommodate the entire universe. It never gets too crowded. There is no traffic jam at the center. There are as many centers as there are individuals. What's more, every individual enjoys a unique center, all to oneself. It is not possible to experience this center as long as the mind clings to faith, reason, or any form of duality that lies (pun intended) at the periphery. A mind that clings to a self-image exists only at the periphery regardless of how brilliant the person, how clever the reasoning, or how strong the faith. Such a mind is torn apart at the periphery by metaphorical centrifugal and centripetal forces of attraction and repulsion.

A logical path from the periphery to the center does not exist. It is, perhaps, what prompted Krishnamurthy to observe that truth is a pathless land, the Zen masters to assert that only no-mind may pass through the gate-less gate to nirvana, and for Jesus to state that it is easier for a camel to go through a needle's eye, than for a rich man to enter the Kingdom of God. The minutest of gaps from the center creates two diametrically opposed polarities such as north-south, good-evil, etc. Sosan (Clark 1984), a Buddhist monk, said "Have no preferences. Make the smallest distinction, however, and heaven and earth are set infinitely apart."

Looked at another way, the center is a point (zero) that contains the whole (infinity). Even skeptical atheists believe that an infinite number of lines converge and vanish into nothingness. And that this zero is directly linked to infinity, its exact antithesis! What a miracle! At the center, all radial lines from the periphery, like the spokes of a wheel, theoretically infinite in number, converge and merge into one point with zero dimensions. Thus, the center is the unmanifest that contains the whole (one, infinite) universe. The zero and one (infinite reality) are engaged in an eternal dance that is governed by the law. The unmanifest self is exactly like the unmanifest Yhwh, Ahura Mazda, or Brahma. No wonder, the Vedic sages ecstatically exclaimed "I am Brahma" (*Aham Brahmasmi*).

It requires introspection and diligent practice to realize the significance of no-self. There are no theological or ideological short cuts. Liberation is possible only at the center where there is no leverage for external forces to manipulate and control no-self (zero). To realize the center (no-self), we need to understand why we cling to the periphery.

Preference (Judgment) at the Periphery

When we cling to a point on the periphery, our perceptions change continuously according to our perceived (social) position. Everything here is relative. A dualistic mind exhibits preferences at the periphery that is made up of opposites: likes-dislikes, great-small, love-hatred, etc., which change with time and circumstances. We experience a restless mind on a roller-coaster ride, which manifests itself as excitement or anxiety. All our judgments exhibit only our preferences or biases. There is a mistaken belief that material wealth, power, fame, etc. will end suffering and bring happiness. It is a mirage that practically everyone seems to be chasing.

Societies focus on abstract values and ideologies but not on individual freedoms. They spend enormous resources to enforce law and order based on their ideologies, which are invariably skewed in support of the wealthy and powerful men who are, usually, very insecure, and fearful of losing their possessions. This has created a gradient that is directed away from the individual center toward the ideological center. People compete against each other to reach it, whereas the *wellness center* is in the exact opposite direction.

The desire and perceived pressure to climb this ladder often lead to lies, deception, stealing, murder, depression, suicide, etc. When we succumb to social pressures, it takes us away from the center toward the periphery where we lead a servile life of compromises, in comparison and coveting, in strife and suffering. It has led to a perennial struggle between the innate nature of people that is in conflict with social values. Some people succumb to the pressures of society and practice deception. One may reach the top of the rung through devious means, but it does not end suffering, nor does it create bliss. The fact that they are constantly surrounded by security guards and retreat to their bunkers at the slightest presence of threat suggests that they are particularly susceptible to a life of fear, anxiety, and insecurity.

Society and organized religions offer preferences at the periphery, but the teachings of the Buddha and Jesus reject any movement toward the periphery. In fact, their teachings take the practitioner in the very opposite direction, away from the periphery, and inward, to the center. Their teachings provide the path of steepest descent to guide us most rapidly to our center, our roots. Sadly, most people reject their teachings and climb the social ladders that take them outward to the periphery, which seems more exciting.

Judgment has no meaning at the center, where both positive and negative simultaneously vanish. Jesus asked his disciples not to judge because judgment indicates a preference at the periphery, which is an incontrovertible proof that the individual is not centered. It is a clear signal for the need to move toward the center.

Even the narrowest path has two diametrically opposite directions. One needs to know the right path as well as the right direction to reach the center. Society has conditioned us to work, compete, and succeed in achieving fame, wealth, and power. All these efforts occur at the periphery. As a result, even expressions like awakening, self-realization, enlightenment, etc., seem to imply the existence of something special that needs to be attained. Since it is seen as an achievement, we tend to look up to those who have accomplished this lofty success. Organized religions have further drilled into us, for good measure, fictitious qualities of such people. We tend to assume it to be beyond the capabilities of the ordinary.

People with awareness have rejected everything at the periphery and dropped to the center where they are no-thing. Instead of climbing the ladder, they have simply jumped off it! Instead of going up, they have gone down. Instead of grabbing, they let go of clinging.

Raised to be a pastor, Nietzsche became an atheistic philosopher instead, when he observed the widespread presence of hypocrisy and bigotry in his society. Having rejected all religions, he sought a rational path to the evolution of a superman with superior qualities. He seems to have perceived and judged life through the filter of a critical thinker in which emotions played a minor role. Ironically, his last act before being diagnosed with insanity was his most compassionate attempt to save a horse from being flogged.

This compassion lay deeply buried within him. He reached the dead-end of logic without recognizing the importance of emotion. He spent much energy on the intellectual judgment of others without realizing his own problems. He did not recognize that what he saw as wrong with the outside world, was a mirror image of what was wrong within himself. He went to the very edge of the precipice. One more step, and he would have fallen right back into his center where he would have discovered his own Buddha-nature. It is sad that he clung to reason, became insane, and died relatively young.

At the center, everything is exactly in balance, there is no preference and no judgment. There is peace and serenity. Connectedness with the infinite gives freedom, eliminates fear, and provides access to endless energy. Love and compassion are experienced as a continuous source of creative energy. Life becomes peaceful, joyful, creative, and naturally fulfilling.

The Barriers to Entry

The barrier to realizing the center is not religion, philosophy, ideology, or science but clinging to a dualistic value system. The ancient sages asked us to focus our efforts on knowing the nature of the true self. Socrates was direct when he instructed, "Know Thyself." Ramana Maharishi, a twentieth-century sage, summed up his teachings in just one question (Maharshi 2016), "Ask yourself: Who am I?" The path of self-inquiry will eventually reveal the truth. Laozi pointed out, "At the center of your being, you have the answer. You know who you are, you know what you need, and nature provides what you need." How difficult could that be!

> *When asked to present his ticket, a passenger became nervous, as he frantically searched in his wallet, suitcase, coat, and pant pockets. Noticing that the passenger had not checked his shirt pocket and trying to be helpful, the conductor asked him to check his shirt pocket, but the passenger turned pale and blurted out, "I can't do that. That is the last place I can look for it. If I don't find it there, then it will mean that I really don't have a ticket!"*

Similarly, we may be afraid of seeing nothing at the center. What will happen if we do not find the truth, nirvana, liberation, self or god at our centers! Life might become meaningless. We may lose motivation to live, which may lead to depression, suicide, or hedonism. We may face contradictions at the periphery, but at least we have hope and excitement. It is a known devil, compared to the unknown angel at the center. We may be unwilling to probe further with logical justifications for our preconceived notions to stay at the periphery and accept its limitations with a "hope for the best" approach. Hence, we accept a life of ups and downs, hoping for more ups and fewer downs. Just like the train passenger, we keep looking outside to keep our hopes alive. Hopes keep us alive and we keep the hopes alive. We could call it a *consolation bias*!

The Nature of the Barriers

We face natural barriers in the form of threats to our body and mind. Our responses take on different forms. When faced with an imminent threat to our physical survival, it is practically all emotions; we may not even have time to think. Reason comes into play only when we have time to think, plan, and act based on past experience and understanding. We need to understand the nature of threats posed to both our bodies and minds and the role of reason and emotion before we move on to *Debugging the Mind*.

In general, we perceive threats at three levels: Gross, Subtle, and Abstract (Table 1).

Level	Threat	Source	Detection
Gross, manifest	External	Fire, Predator,...	Sensory Organs
Subtle, manifest	Internal-physical	Pathogens,...	Scientific Tools
Abstract, unmanifest	Internal-mental	Ignorance	Mind

Table 1. Threat Levels & Responses

At the gross level, threats to our survival and physical wellbeing appear in the form of predators, floods, fire, etc. They are detected by sensory organs and sensory-motor functions respond to them based on instincts, past experience, and memory. For example, if we were to encounter a snake, our sensory organs would almost instantly recognize it and the fight-or-flight options immediately kick into play. Progress in science and technology has greatly minimized risks from gross threats.

Our ability to sense the external world is limited to gross objects, but science has shown that matter also exists at levels that our sense organs cannot detect. Pathogens, microorganisms, atoms, molecules, sub-atomic matter, electric current, nuclear radiation, electromagnetism, etc. that exist at subtle levels could cause serious damage. We depend on science and technology to protect ourselves from subtle threats.

We have made enormous progress with regard to gross and subtle threats, but abstract threats are the most ominous and insidious. They are invisible and neither sensory organs nor current scientific tools can detect them. Abstract threats come in the forms of symbols, images, and ideas that suggest explicit or implicit harm to individuals and groups. When these abstract threats are perceived as real and converted into actions in the form of violent conflicts and wars, they spread immense suffering.

Identification of the self with images based on race, caste, tribe, ethnicity, religion, nationality, etc. plays a major role in perpetuating this problem, as any real or perceived disrespect for them often leads to violent retaliation. The diabolical nature of such threats creates fear, anxiety, and insecurity, which lead to actions that range from petty arguments to hate crimes, terrorism, and wars. They have created suspicion, mutual distrust, animosity, bias, and hatred across the globe.

Mental suffering arises from an adverse relationship between the image of the self and the other in one's own brain. An image, by definition, is not real. A photograph, e.g., is an image of the real object that is projected on a screen or paper. What is projected in our brain is also an image. An image by itself does not cause any harm, but suffering is caused by actions that are based on false perceptions of reality (ignorance).

False Perceptions of Reality

Physical and psychological illusions play a key role in creating false perceptions of reality.

For example, a two-dimensional image of a staircase that appears to go up and away suddenly flips to appear as if it is descending toward us. The front face of an image of a cube instantly flips into its interior side. An interesting feature of such illusions is that we are able to visualize only one of the two possibilities at any given instant even though we know that both possibilities co-exist. It is like an on-off switch, one or the other but not both or anything in between. The cube may appear facing us or the other way; the stairs may be ascending away from us or descending toward us but not both simultaneously. And, nothing in between. The switch happens naturally, instantly, and involuntarily.

It is impossible to convince others of the existence of an illusion unless they have seen it, in which case there is no need to convince them. It is not based on faith. Either one knows or doesn't. The only way to recognize it is to observe it directly. It may take a bit of effort, concentration, playfulness, and relaxation but eventually, it suddenly strikes us.

Similarly, we become aware of a psychological illusion only when we realize it. Until then, no one can be convinced of its existence. We have to keep making diligent effort.

Psychological illusions are subtler than physical illusions. We are able to recognize a physical illusion by comparing the original with its image, but it is difficult to recognize psychological illusions that are related to abstract thoughts. Just as a two-dimensional projection of a real three-dimensional object creates two possible solutions and we are able to perceive only one of them at a time, a real individual creates two images in our mind, based on dualistic values: friend or foe, good or evil, etc. The mind then clings to one of them as real although it is only a possibility and not a certainty. Clinging to one of them as real could result in violent conflicts when the actions of others are also based on illusory images.

Illusion (*maya*) is a common theme in Hindu philosophy and *advaita* is its main contribution. *Advaita* means, "not-two." Our mind splits reality into two: the other and I.

One might wonder why the Vedic sages did not talk about *one* reality instead of negating two. They did so because, even if they spoke of one, the listener would still think of two realities: an exalted reality of the sage and the mundane reality of the listener. Hence, they chose negation as a way to describe reality, leaving no wiggle room for the disciple to obfuscate it. They made it even more mysterious with statements like, "You are that (*Tat Tvam Asi*)" and "I am that (*Aham Brahmasmi*)." It was an unambiguous way of conveying that we are not different from reality.

Whether the illusion is physical or psychological in nature, we need a frame of reference to figure it out. In the case of drunkenness, it is the sober state that acts as a reference. In the case of a dream, it is the waking state that defines it. In the case of two-dimensional images of physical objects, it is the original three-dimensional object that serves as the reference. We need the original mind to recognize the psychological illusion. The Zen masters called it the no-mind or the *original face*. The only way to realize it is to be one. Also, just as we cannot describe the waking state to an individual who is fast asleep, it is not possible to describe the awakened state to an individual with a dualistic mind that mistakes the illusory perception for real.

It is important to recognize how psychological illusions play a major role in human interactions. We perceive each other as an abstract image (engineer, student, teacher, friend, father, mother, daughter, son, husband, wife, Chinese, American, Christian, Muslim, black, white, brown, etc.) Problems get compounded when the image is qualified by abstract values (e.g., good-evil, superior-inferior, right-wrong, moral-immoral, ugly-beautiful, loving-hateful, trustworthy-duplicitous, etc.) We are mentally conditioned to look at each other according to a preconceived profile based on association (memory) and current desires.

Just as we cannot be sure from a picture whether it is an ascending or descending flight of stairs, we cannot know, *a priori* or even in real-time, whether a person has good or evil intentions, is a saint or a sinner, etc. Biases based on race, religion, gender, looks, dress, wealth, power, scholarship, etc., have taken deep roots in the human psyche. It is this combination of biased images and a belief in arbitrary dualistic values that is the primary cause of illusion. *Psychological interactions take place between abstract images. What we perceive of the other is the image of the other. We never truly "know" the other.*

People commit evil acts not because they are innately evil or because Satan is directing them, but because they are clinging to images that cause fear, anxiety, and insecurity. They are fighting a phantom but sadly, others do the same, which makes everything look normal. We are like the prisoners in Plato's *Allegory of the Cave* (Jowett 2017). It is practically impossible to convince anyone to the contrary when the concerned person is under the influence of an illusion that is apparently built on past history, profiling, and perceived threats.

Evil acts are the result of ghosts fighting other ghosts. *The ghost is within us, not in the lamppost,* and it cannot be evicted by an external authority, as we are the only one with access to our mind. Organized religions and non-religious ideologies have misled humanity down a rabbit hole by giving these images fictitious meanings and purposes. To get out of the rabbit hole, we must recognize the limitation of dualistic language and how it causes illusory (false) perceptions of reality within our own minds, as the answer also is within us.

Linguistic Obfuscation

In stark contrast to the language of nature, which is silent, unique, unambiguous, invariant, and absolute, human language is loud, dualistic, ambiguous, variable, and relative. It leads to logical obfuscation. Linguistic obfuscation has allowed precious precepts and teachings to be converted into arbitrary morals and deceptive religious practices. Instead of blindly accepting religious interpretations, one must seek intuitive understanding of the precepts and teachings. Such an understanding will come only through practice but not through intellectual catechisms.

How linguistic obfuscation could lead to erroneous conclusions is illustrated with the following examples from fiction. It is meant to suggest that esoteric doctrines, mythical beings, miracles, and morals could belong to the same category.

Alice Through the Looking Glass (Carroll 1999)

In this humorous episode, Lewis Carroll made brilliant obfuscation of the word 'nobody.'

The King said, "I haven't seen the two Messengers, either. They've both gone to the town. Just look along the road and tell me if you can see either of them."

"I see nobody on the road," said Alice.

"I only wish I had such eyes," the King remarked in a fretful tone. "To be able to see Nobody! And at that distance, too! Why, it's as much as I can do to see real people, by this light!"

Later, when one of the Messengers had returned, the King went on, "Who did you pass on the road?" holding out his hand to the Messenger for some more hay.

"Nobody," said the Messenger.

"Quite so," said the King: "this young lady saw him too. So, of course, Nobody walks much slower than you"

"I do my best," the Messenger said in a sulky tone. "I'm sure nobody walks faster than I do!"

"He can't do that," said the King, "or else he'd have been here first. However, now you've got your breath, you may tell us what's happened in the town."

Odyssey (Palmer 1892)

In Homer's epic *Odyssey*, Odysseus obfuscated in the exact opposite manner by referring to himself as *Nobody* to escape from Polyphemus, a giant single-eyed Cyclops.

When Odysseus arrived at the island of Cyclops on his way to Ithaca, Polyphemus trapped Odysseus and his men in a cave and ate a few of his men.

The next day, when Polyphemus returned to the cave, Odysseus gave him some strong wine to drink. The giant thanked him profusely for the great treat and asked what his name was.

Odysseus responded, "Nobody."

Being grateful and drunk, Polyphemus went into a deep sleep. Odysseus grabbed a wooden stake and blinded Polyphemus' single eye.

Hearing his screams, other Cyclops came rushing and asked him, "Who did this to you?"

Polyphemus responded, "Nobody."

Thinking that he was out of his senses or that some god has attacked him, the Cyclops left. As Polyphemus was blind, Odysseus and his remaining men escaped from the island.

Uncle Dynamite (Wodehouse 1948)

Let us look at another example, a funny episode in *Uncle Dynamite* a novel by my most favorite author P.G. Wodehouse.

Constable Potter was reporting the matter of someone pushing him into the duck pond.

"I was assaulted by the duck pond, sir."

"By the duck pond?" Sir Aylmer echoed, his eyes widening.

"Yes, sir," responded the Constable.

"How the devil can you be assaulted by a duck pond?" asked Sir Aylmer, incredulously.

"When I said that I was assaulted by the duck pond, Sir, I did not mean that I was assaulted by the duck pond, but that I was assaulted by the duck pond," answered the Constable patiently.

Inferno (Alighieri 1899)

I was in the midst of a serious after-dinner conversation at home with a friend, Harry (now deceased), a retired executive from a major aerospace company. The topic somehow drifted toward a serious discussion of Dante's *Inferno*.

Harry conveyed that according to Dante, the inscription on the first gate to hell was, "Abandon hope all ye who enter here."

I had not read Dante, but when I heard his explanation, I burst out laughing, which seemed to upset Harry. He asked me what was so funny about it.

I said, "I see reality to be the exact opposite. In fact, I see 'Abandon all hope,' as the first and only step to heaven. Hope is what we carry with us to our grave. It is pure fiction, the most addictive drug that makes us cling to it in the belief that everything will work out well. As we also know that everything may not work out as hoped, clinging to hope leads to fear and anxiety, a living hell. Thus, one could state that not abandoning, but *clinging to hope is the first step to hell*. We become free by learning to accept life as a present and living in the present. To feel blessed and thankful for what nature has given us unconditionally and living with no concern for the future, is heaven. 'Abandon all hope' (in flawed social values) is the first and only step to heaven! Getting out of the rat race and being human is the only step."

Thus, even a profound statement could be rationally interpreted in two diametrically opposite ways, with both making logical sense. When he heard my interpretation, he was ecstatic, and gave me a high-five. A few years later when I visited him in Denver, he said that his friends liked it when he took the liberty of explaining it my way to them.

Pithy Statements by the Buddha, Jesus, and Socrates

Did the Buddha mean that there was no self or that there *was* no-self? Did Muhammad say that there was no god or that there *was* no-god?

Let us briefly review how some statements made by the Buddha, Jesus, and Socrates could be logically misconstrued. It is meant to suggest that there is a need to pause, reflect, and intuitively realize what makes absolute sense, and not be carried away by a biased but logical meaning.

The Buddha said that ignorance is the cause of suffering, Jesus said truth liberates, and Socrates said that "no one knowingly and willingly does any wrong." However, the words *ignorance*, *truth*, and *wrong* are undefined.

Ignorance is invariably interpreted in an intellectual manner, as a lack of knowledge. Modern philosophers incorrectly refer to nirvana as supreme concentration. Supreme concentration requires a mind, whereas nirvana is the absence of a self-image, it is no-self, no-mind.

Jesus probably meant *truth* in an absolute sense. Jesus's truth could be a reference to direct awareness of one's innate nature that obliterates all intellectual obstacles to liberation. Religious interpretation of his statement is invariably intellectual, using dualistic logic. Theologians have interpreted liberation to mean many different things based on the concept of a supernatural God. They have also created unverifiable and unfalsifiable concepts of heaven and hell.

Plato (Segvic 2000), perhaps unwittingly but logically, took exception to Socrates' observation, "no one knowingly and willing does any wrong." He contradicted Socrates by pointing out that tyrants knowingly and willingly do wrong when they exile or kill people. He suggested that Socrates' observation was true only for those who exercised self-control based on moral values (virtues). However, Socrates probably meant that an individual, like himself, who was aware of the true nature of reality, cannot intentionally do any wrong.

Plato and Aristotle developed the concept of virtue based on reason, which has plagued the West for millennia because man-made morals do not have a verifiable (or falsifiable), uniformly valid, universally acceptable, inviolable, and invariant frame of reference. It allowed rulers to define and impose values that are heavily biased in their favor to control and exploit others.

As the statements made by the Buddha, Jesus, and Socrates render themselves to non-unique interpretation, theologians, religious followers, and philosophers were able to weave any story that sounded logical according to their convenience and social (tribal) conditioning.

As linguistic obfuscations could go either way, it is also possible to logically show that the statements made by the Buddha, Jesus, and Socrates are not profound but trivial.

We could be either ignorant or aware of the true nature of reality. If we are ignorant, i.e. if our perception of reality is false, then we tend to blindly stumble and suffer the consequences. Thus, it is practically tautological to state that ignorance is the cause of suffering, and nobody would knowingly or willingly do any wrong. On the other hand, if we are aware of the true nature of reality, we can clearly see and, naturally, avoid the pitfalls, and be free. It is obvious that the truth liberates. Thus, the statements made by the Buddha, Jesus, and Socrates could be logically interpreted as: "if you are blind, you are likely to stumble, fall, and suffer, but if you have eyes, you can see and be free (not to stumble)." They are hardly profound.

When we are in a rabbit hole, our perception of reality can be flawed and illusory. The image of *one* conjures up the image of *none*. *Nobody* could be a Nobody or the absence of a person. Emptiness and the whole are inseparable. Dualism is inherent in logic, language, morals, and our perception of reality, but reality is not two. Dualistic logic and language divide the absolute into two mutually exclusive parts but, as the Vedic Rishis pointed out, reality is 'not-two.'

This fundamental limitation of language and logic must be recognized before one can realize the insights conveyed by the Buddha, Jesus, Socrates, Vedic Rishis, and others regarding the true nature of reality. One could become aware of it but, to repeat, a logical path to realizing it does not exist. It is one or the other: either we are ignorant, or we are aware of the truth. We can either see the illusion or not see it. Any attempt to interpret the absolute in dualistic terms will miss the truth. To paraphrase Vedic sages, "Truth (reality) is not-two (*advaita*)."

Dualistic interpretation of their insights has played a tragic role in creating a vast gap between precepts and practices. In practice, it allowed precepts of love, forgiveness, and mercy for the loved ones to be converted into hatred, vengeance, and cruelty toward those who are perceived as enemies. Such transformations occurred not because the rulers and religious followers were unfamiliar with the meaning of these words. They logically defined their values (morals) to suit their selfish interests.

For example, the Ten Commandments forbids killing. With a sleight of hand, killing animals was permitted but only murder was prohibited. With vigorous flag-waving, the killing of thousands was not only permitted but glorified when it was carried out with an accompaniment of trumpets (Redman 1949). People justify their actions to receive rewards or face rebuke and punishment. Actions based on such disingenuous interpretations create discord in *feelings, thoughts, words, and actions*, which manifests in the form of hypocrisy and bigotry.

The only way to realize the true nature of reality is through direct intuitive understanding.

The Limitations of Traditional Approaches

Theology and non-religious ideologies like communism share a common characteristic: both are based on dualistic logic however tenuous it might be. Their doctrines and values (morals, ethical principles) are based on logic and reason that lack a uniformly valid, invariant, and inviolable frame of reference. In the absence of such a reference, it is not difficult for the rich and powerful to mold logic and reason to suit their interests and enforce them with physical force.

There is a tendency to assume that science and critical thinking will eliminate suffering. However, this is not supported by available evidence. Education and critical thinking are necessary, but not sufficient to eliminate emotional problems.

Historically, scientific research has invariably been funded by rulers. Even the airfoil that I designed was used in the design of military aircraft that are used to drop bombs. Philosophers, scientists, and engineers have played key roles in wars that killed millions of people and in maintaining law and order in societies based on racism, casteism, religion, slavery, segregation, etc. We drop bombs that maim or kill thousands, including women, children, patients, and Doctors without Borders. We callously call it collateral damage. They are planned and executed by highly qualified people with scientific and technological expertise. Atrocities like the Holocaust, gulags and dropping of bombs were not carried out by people who lacked religious backgrounds, scientific expertise, philosophical erudition, or critical thinking. We can only conclude that we carry out such atrocities due to some kind of collective mental sickness.

I lived for almost four years in Moscow, in the former Soviet Union. Both my wife and I were treated with great warmth and friendliness. There was no fear of violence at any time of the day or night, but I also encountered many shortcomings in that society. Even simple problems could not be resolved easily. It looked as though every initiative needed approval from the Kremlin. Lack of freedom was evident. Fear, anxiety, and insecurity ruled their lives.

They certainly had a better standard of living than that I was used to in India, but I had come across more smiling faces and laughter even in the slums of Mumbai than on the streets of Moscow, where people seemed to carry a heavy burden on their shoulders. I felt sad because, although their existential needs were taken care of, they had so little freedom. Suppression of individual freedom was one of their biggest drawbacks. When creativity is curbed, life becomes drab, and devoid of joy. Communism, as I saw it, worshiped the hammer and sickle that symbolized the rule by proletariat (working-class), but the power still rested in the hands of a few (sometimes one dictator).

Nazi Germany under fascism was not lacking in scientists or philosophers and was on the verge of developing its own nuclear bomb. Hitler himself was a critical thinker, presumably with a high IQ. A large number of highly qualified engineers and intellectuals executed his plans. Some of the most brilliant scientists, philosophers, and critical thinkers, including well-known Nobel laureates, passively or actively supported Nazi atrocities.

Those who dropped atom bombs on Hiroshima and Nagasaki, which maimed or killed hundreds of thousands of innocent people were not irrational. Everything was well-planned and executed with the participation of Noble laureates, scientists, engineers, and erudite scholars. The Soviet Union punished millions with hard labor in gulags, while their scientists, intellectuals, and philosophers passively watched in dismay or actively participated in the mayhem. History has witnessed similar behavior from the followers of all religions and ideologies.

For millennia, religion was viewed as the final authority on morals (Sagi 1995). Theologians, priests and rulers claim that morals were conveyed by

God *himself* but they themselves violate them without compunction. The behavior of followers of the same religion, with the same professed moral values, varies across a wide range, from saints to psychopaths, and sexual predators. Every religion has splintered into numerous denominations that engage in sectarian conflicts. In addition, there have been perennial conflicts between the followers of various religions. Societies based on capitalism, socialism, communism, fascism, monarchy, democracy, and dictatorship are involved in conflicts against each other, as their values are not identical. Conflicts caused by differing perceived values exist across the board, down to personal friendship and marriage.

For millennia, religions and ideologies have used rewards and punishments to impose man-made morals to control feelings, words, and actions, which have resulted in endless suffering.

As morals lack a uniformly valid and invariant frame of reference (Hutcheson 2015), and as societal norms vary from one culture to another, strangers, who do not share a common moral framework that provides the basis for the resolution of conflicts, may find each other as acting out of mutually exclusive values that might even appear barbaric (Boas 1962) (Engelhardt 1991). McIntyre has described the problem thus: "*It is a central feature of contemporary moral debates that they are unsettlable and interminable* (Callahan 1981)."

Debugging the Mind makes moral debates irrelevant with the recognition that the innate nature of all human beings is the same. In general, *every individual has a natural preference for physical and mental wellbeing and an aversion for pain and suffering.* That is our natural *moral* value. We are born with it. We are happy when we fulfill this natural need and refrain from causing pain and suffering to others, as they too share the same natural values.

Part II, which follows next, is devoted to *Debugging the Mind,* a systematic three-phase approach to meet this natural need and lead a free, fearless, and fulfilling life.

PART II

Debugging the Mind

5

The Three-Phase Approach

What is that, if it is known, by which everything is revealed?
—**Mundaka Upanishad** *(Krishnananda 1951)*

My uncle, a mathematics professor, and I were having a heated argument about the correct solution to a set of complex differential equations. My aunt, who came in to find out what the commotion was about, looked over our shoulders, laughed, and said, "I notice that all the equations have a zero on the right-hand side of the equal sign. The answer is obviously zero! What are you quarreling about?"

Her stunning revelation ended the argument and we almost split our ribs from the ensuing laughter. In scientific research, we usually seek the unknown solution to a known problem, but my aunt pointed out the very opposite: the exact solution is known. How to realize it is the real problem. Her insight is especially valid for *Debugging the Mind.*

Newton conveyed one of the most profound insights with his third law: "*action and reaction are equal and opposite.*" As they are exactly balanced, their sum is zero. If one is known, the other is naturally revealed. The existence of balance in physical processes emerges from this law. Laws of conservation of mass, momentum, and energy, which laid the foundation for the spectacular success of modern science, are all based on balance.

Newton's laws govern the dynamics of the objective world, but the mind is an emergent, metaphysical phenomenon and not a physical object. However, it exhibits some characteristics that resemble a dynamic system. For example, we describe its trajectory and *e-motion* with words like excited, crestfallen, agitated, floating on cloud nine, depressed, etc. Thus, one could surmise that, like the body, the mind too could lose balance, become unstable, experience a metaphorical fall, and suffer the consequences.

Practically all traditional religions focus on the problem and merely hope to realize the mythical solution either in this life or in the afterlife. However, they have an airtight logic to deter doubters with "heads I win, tails you lose" approach. Even Pascal, the great mathematician, scientist, and philosopher, betted on the existence of God, which is known as 'Pascal's wager' (Houston 1984). He observed that happiness was an illusion and misery was the norm. Many people are resigned to this perception of reality with the 'hope for the best' approach.

In stark contrast, *Debugging the Mind* aims to eliminate mental disturbances and realize mental balance in this life, here and now. And for good. We may not have experienced nirvana or liberation, but we know what is hurting us. Some problems are intense, and others are merely annoying. They may appear in the shape of a supercilious boss, a cheating partner, a bossy mother-in-law, an abusive husband, a nagging wife, a condescending relative, a religious bigot, a racist neighbor, someone jumping the queue or cutting us off on the highway, and various physical and mental threats. They may be too many to list or remember. They lurk somewhere within the mind until they suddenly emerge and cause stress.

It might appear that we have no control over others, but the focus is not on controlling them, becoming resilient, or clamming up. *The objective of Debugging the Mind is to understand our innate nature and lead a fearless, playful, and creative life regardless of the external factors.*

Objectives of Debugging the Mind

The purpose of *Debugging the Mind* is succinctly described by the following secular verse from *Brihadaranyaka Upanishad* (Madhavananda 2015), which was compiled around 700 BCE. Large sections of the work are devoted to the understanding of the mind.

In a delightful conversation between the Rishi Yajnavalkya and his wife Maitreyi, one of the greatest woman-philosophers of yore, the author describes the nature of our mind. Through them, the author explains that everything we do is for our own sake. We love others for our own sake. Even so-called altruism is for our own sake. We care for others for our own sake. A mother takes care of her child for her own sake. She does not see the baby as other but as a part of herself. He was suggesting that all of us possess this kind of innate nature. Our mind seeks fulfillment in being one with nature, which we see as the other. We feel happy and peaceful when it is realized. The purpose of this invocation is to realize it.

This invocation seeks a return to our innate nature, where everything we do is for our own sake, which naturally turns out to be good for *others* too. It is how nature has designed us. When such awareness is realized, there is no room for suffering. Peace settles in us.

The words on the right are the Sanskrit version of the invocation.

Lead me

From Falsehood to Truth	*Asato maa sadgamaya*
From Ignorance to Awareness	*Tamaso maa jyotirgamaya*
From Death to Immortality	*Mrityo maa amritamgamaya*
(Let there be) Peace, Peace, Peace.	*Om shaanti, shaanti, shaantih.*

The invocation may seem to be seeking guidance from a mythical external agent, but both the seeker and the sought are the same. As mentioned earlier, even if we worship God, the image of God exists only within us. We might as well be honest about it and try to directly understand reality.

Falsehood, truth, ignorance, awareness, death, and deathlessness are ideas that we entertain in our head. Mental disturbances are caused when we cling to falsehood. So, we seek truth. Mental suffering is caused by our actions that are carried out in ignorance. So, we seek awareness. Death causes fear and anxiety. So, we seek freedom from death (immortality).

The author of this invocation was not referring to immortality as an anti-dote to physical death. It would be hypocritical to seek an end to falsehood and ignorance in the first two lines and then offer a myth (falsehood or ignorance) as a solution.

Falsehood, ignorance, and death are all related to our self-image (ego), which does not have a physical existence. When we give credence to our self-image in ignorance, it creates its own world view with myths and miracles that do not match reality. When we let go of our clinging to the imaginary self-image, awareness of truth would liberate us from mental disturbances and suffering. Self-image is like a ghost in the lamppost: it is neither born nor destroyed. It exists only as long as we believe in it. Death has no meaning in the absence of a self-image. This realization eliminates the fear of death. Peace naturally settles in us once and for all.

Fundamental Principles

Debugging the Mind is not based on fiction, but on facts that are known to every individual, without having to depend on an external authority. If the desired goal is freedom, we must start with freedom and stick with it. If the desired goal is truth, we must start with the truth and stick with it. It may appear tough in the beginning, but progress will be rapid when we stick with it.

Truth and freedom are our innate nature. We have been socially conditioned to embrace falsehood. *Debugging the Mind* is a three-phase approach to realizing our innate nature based on the following two principles:

> **The First Principle**: *Do not do to others what we would not want others to do to us.*
>
> **The Second Principle**: *Maintain feelings, thoughts, words, and actions in harmony.*

The first principle is the well-known Hillel-Kongzi Golden Rule, which is the basic tenet of all major religions. Not harming others in thoughts as well as deeds is a unilateral decision that is completely within the control and capability of an individual. It is not a moral injunction, but a prophylactic measure to prevent mental disturbances (bugs) from taking root in the mind. The first principle is the *necessary condition* that must be fulfilled in order to realize liberation.

Mental suffering would vanish from the face of the earth if everyone diligently practiced the first principle. For millennia, people have been individually and collectively violating the first principle through deception, treachery, abusive behavior, rape, murder, hate crimes, and wars in which millions are maimed, displaced, and killed. They may have infected the whole world with mental sickness, but every individual has the innate ability to maintain mental wellbeing by implementing the first principle.

Although the first principle is innately known, fear, anxiety, insecurity, covetousness, anger, hatred, etc. can persuade an individual to violate it. Even such simple acts as jumping the queue, using slurs, parking in the wrong place, not wearing a face mask during a pandemic, etc. have caused violent reactions, including shooting and death. It is hard to remain unaffected when we are confronted with aggressive behavior, lest we be mistaken for a weakling. It takes courage and commitment to consistently fulfill the first principle. The meaning, purpose, and implementation of the first principle are described in the next chapter on **prevention**.

The second principle, viz., "*Maintain feelings, thoughts, words, and actions in harmony*" is the *sufficiency condition* for realizing mental freedom. As with the first principle, the contents of the second principle are also innately known to every individual. Everyone can recognize the presence of discord among one's own *feelings, thoughts, words, and actions*, but perceived adversarial forces cause mental disturbances. It is the crux of the problem.

The second principle simultaneously provides a qualitative feedback to monitor progress. The intensity of discord among feelings, thoughts, words, and actions is known (e.g., small, tolerable, intolerable, etc., on a scale of one to ten). As all the parameters (feelings, thoughts, words and actions) are affected by unpredictable external sources, it is difficult to maintain harmony among them during the initial stages of this effort. The nature of mental disturbances is explored through meditative practices that are described in Chapter 7 on **exploration**.

Mental disturbances tend to persist even after long periods of meditation, albeit at a much lower level compared to the initial state. *Debugging the Mind* describes three distinct techniques in Chapter 8 on **experimentation** to eliminate mental disturbances in toto, once and for all.

The Three-Phase Approach

Debugging the Mind is carried out in three phases (Fig. 5.1) (S. Mangalam 2018).

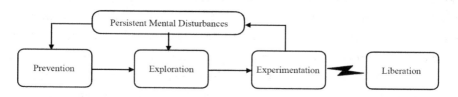

Figure 5.1. The Three-Phase Approach for Debugging the Mind.

1. Phase I: **Prevention** of mental disturbances from taking root in the mind;
2. Phase II: **Exploration** of the mind to identify the nature of existing mental disturbances; and
3. Phase III: **Experimentation** to eradicate mental disturbances and realize liberation.

Prevention is a prophylactic measure based on the first principle, viz., *do not do to others what you do not want others to do to you*. It is a unilateral attitude, regardless of what others do. It does not state that we should do no harm only if others don't. There are no ifs and no buts.

Practice of the first principle, viz., *do not do to others what you do not want others to do to you*, leads to vital insights about one's own state of mind. For example, deliberate actions aimed at harming others are carried out only by those who are unhappy. An emotionally fulfilled individual would not intentionally harm anyone. In other words, if we try to intentionally harm anyone, it is a sure indication that we are already suffering. Strict adherence to the first principle will make us stop in our tracks and focus on getting rid of our ailment instead of inflicting pain on others. *We cannot get rid of our stomachache by giving others a headache.*

It may be best to begin the practice of the first principle with small steps in a relatively safe and supportive environment like home, school, or a monastery to first realize an emotionally stable mind before venturing out to practice in society. It is best instilled in a child.

The objective of **exploration** in Phase II is to conduct self-diagnosis to identify the nature of existing mental disturbances.

Patanjali addressed this problem in *Ashtanga Yoga Sutra* (Ranganathan 2014), which is a succinct manual for understanding the body-mind-emotion coupling as a means to create mental balance. *Debugging the Mind* adopts his approach for the **exploration** of the mind. It begins with ten precepts (*yama and niyama*), followed by physical exercise (popularly known as yoga) to maintain a supple body, and breathing exercises (*pranayama*) to understand the body-emotion coupling. The next three steps are devoted to meditative techniques (*pratyahara, dharana, and dhyana*) to understand emotion-mind coupling.

These seven steps are designed to reveal the nature of mental disturbances. Patanjali does not explain how mental balance is realized at the end of the seventh step. Some seekers may intuitively realize mental balance at this stage, just as some children learn to ride a bicycle even without the help of the training wheels.

Research has shown that yoga and meditation have a profound calming effect on the mind, but mental disturbances can persist even after prolonged practice. An intellectual path to bridge this gap and attain complete mental balance (samadhi, nirvana, or liberation) does not exist.

Experimentation in Phase III is devoted to bridging this gap.

As described in Chapter 3, there are four natural paths to liberation that are tailored to meet the specific needs of individuals with *thinking, feeling, sensing,* or *intuition* as the dominant cognitive function. Patanjali's *Yoga Sutra* will suffice for those with *intuition* as the dominant cognitive function. The chapter on **experimentation** describes three distinct paths for those with *thinking, feeling, or sensing* as their dominant cognitive function.

Nirvana or liberation is a revelation that occurs like a lightning bolt, akin to scientific discoveries or how a child suddenly realizes physical balance to ride a bicycle. It is an intuitive realization of mental balance and wellbeing when mental disturbances completely vanish.

6

Prevention

Prevention is better than cure.
—**Desiderius Erasmus** *(Tracy 2019)*

Prevention, as the word implies, is a prophylactic measure to maintain a healthy mind and avoid actions that create mental disturbances in the form of fear, anxiety, and insecurity.

The Significance of the First Principle

Prevention is based on practicing the first principle: *Do not do to others what we would not like others to do to us*, which is the essence of the precepts of major religions.

The first principle, *do not do to others what we would not like others to do to us*, is self-evident and does not depend on scriptural knowledge, scientific expertise, or external authority. It is not a moral injunction. It is, in fact, the innate nature of mentally healthy and emotionally fulfilled individuals. It is a mutual need of all human beings.

The first principle emerges from the fundamental understanding that *every individual has a natural preference for physical and mental wellbeing and an aversion for pain and suffering*. Practically all mental suffering is caused by people who violate this principle. We begin *Debugging the Mind* by making a unilateral decision to respect the needs of others just as we expect others to respect ours. As described in the following chapters, diligent adherence to the first principle paradoxically helps us realize our own mental wellbeing.

The first principle is a fundamental precept that was designed by the ancient sages to maintain a healthy mind. It is not based on inviolable laws of nature. We can violate it at will. Nature does not prevent us from telling lies, cheating, stealing, killing, coveting, or committing adultery. Violating the first principle, however, is no different from eating toxic food or drinking polluted water; we are bound to get hurt sooner or later. Even if we were a Michelangelo, it would be impossible to do our masterpiece in an inebriated state on a leaky boat in stormy seas. We need an able body, a calm mind, and a clean environment to lead a healthy and creative life.

A literal interpretation of the first principle without a profound understanding of its purpose could be misleading. For example, some actions like surgery may cause pain, but the doctor's intention is not to hurt but to heal. When parents discipline their child to acquire various skills, the child may initially resent it, but eventually realizes the benefit. We do physical exercise that may be painful, but it ensures robust physical health. Such actions are motivated by a benefit to the recipient in the long run, but not to cause needless pain or harm. All actions that emerge from care, compassion, and kindness naturally fulfill the first principle.

The first principle is simple and straightforward. It is not asking us to climb Mt. Everest or swim across an ocean. It does not ask us to be truthful only if all others are truthful. We must be truthful even if the rest of the world is lying. We mustn't cheat even if everyone else is deceiving. It is independent of other people. It is absolute. It is for our own good.

Any problem that we might face in fulfilling the first principle has nothing to do with others. The source of the problem is within us and so is the solution. Doubts about others are only an attempt to justify a short-term solution, an attempt to escape personal responsibility, and unwillingness to adhere to this principle. What we need is a commitment to diligent practice. *Without practice, the* first principle *is merely an intellectual exercise.*

At the gross level, damage caused by physical actions is immediately known. For example, if we were to jump off a cliff, the results would be swift and practically instantaneous. At the subtle level, a physical illness caused by bacteria, viruses, toxic food, etc. may take some time to manifest itself. Compared to them, it is very difficult to recognize the existence of a correlation between the violation of the first principle and its consequences, as the time-delay is usually very large. Scientific proof for its veracity does not exist. It is a heuristic.

It may appear that clever people get away with murder, but they are easily rattled by the presence of unfettered individuals. It means that deceptive people carry festering wounds that get exposed in the presence of free individuals.

Fear and freedom are irreconcilable.

A naked Diogenes walked free with an emotionally contented mind whereas the powerful but discontented king Alexander needed a legion to protect him.

Fear makes rulers surround themselves with secrecy, security forces, and sycophants. Driven by fear, they poisoned Socrates, nailed Jesus, and persecuted Muhammad, who were gentle people. It might have been crude in the past and sophisticated now, but rulers live in fear, anxiety, and insecurity all their lives. Mental suffering, emotional insecurity, and many types of physical and psychosomatic ailments are the price people pay for violating the first principle.

Compassion naturally arises within us when we realize that anyone who is trying to harm us is already suffering. It is similar to our attitude toward someone who is suffering from physical disease or injury. It may not always be possible to help them, but, at least, we could sympathize and not despise them. There is a possibility, however small, that with time, they may change for the better and learn from the experience of seeing no negative impact of their behavior on us. It is up to nature to decide that!

Tirukkural (Sundaram 2005), a compendium of 1330 couplets that were composed nearly two millennia ago by the Tamil poet Tiruvalluvar, addressed this problem in ten couplets, most of which went farther than the Hillel-Kongzi Golden Rule. He offered antidotes to harm done to us by others. One of those couplets advised, "when others hurt you, do something good for them in return and help them realize their mistake and correct themselves."

Violation of the first principle allows false perceptions of reality to take root in the mind and spread over time in the form of depression, guilt, anger, hatred, etc., which could lead to homicide, suicide and major wars. It might cause post-traumatic stress disorder (PTSD) as a result of unconsciously causing harm to innocent people. In stark contrast, the mind becomes peaceful and a source of joy when the first principle is consistently practiced.

It is relatively easy to implement the first principle when the *other* is a loved one. It is challenging only outside one's close circle, where everyone appears to be jostling against each other to get ahead of the game by hook or by crook. Lacking courage, many people succumb to temptations and violate the first principle, which leads to a vicious cycle and a life of suffering.

As the practice of the first principle entails some risks in the adversarial social order, it may be prudent to begin cautiously in safe surroundings where we are not troubled by the need to compete with others. The best option may be to do so at home, in the safe environment of the family. It is best if the first principle is inculcated in children before they are exposed to the outside world. Once we learn how to swim or ride a bicycle, the skill stays with us for life. The same is true with the first principle.

We could also practice the first principle in a safe external environment like a monastery or *ashram*. A good teacher is invaluable. The Zen monastery in Sogenji, Japan, where I spent several months, is a good example of such a place. Of course, it is best to be courageous, steadfast, and face the problem head-on in society. It is also the most effective path.

The Ten Commandments and the Precepts of Yoga

Prevention of mental disturbances is most effectively realized by implementing the Ten Commandments or the ten Yama and Niyama of yoga, as described in this section. *Precepts are addressed to the individual.* They are not meant for preaching to the choir on weekends. They are meant to be implemented in daily life. *Every one of them is self-evident and within the control and innate authority of an individual to implement.*

We begin with the Ten Commandments.

The Ten Commandments

The Ten Commandments (Barclay 1998) prevent falsehood from taking root in our mind and prepare us to meet the challenges of life with strength, freedom, joy, creativity, and compassion. We could look at them as the preparation of soil for sowing seeds that will eventually become an emotionally fulfilling, fruit-bearing tree of life. *They create the Garden of Eden within us.*

The first three commandments describe the nature of creation: The trinity of the *unmanifest*, the *manifest* creation, and the law (*davar*, word, or shariah) that governs creation. The next two commandments give instructions for maintaining a healthy body and mind. The last five are devoted to the **prevention** of falsehood from taking root in the mind.

1. You shall have no gods before me.

Expressed in a symbolic manner, Yhwh is the *unmanifest* origin of the *manifest* creation. Just as zero is the origin of the coordinate system, Yhwh exists as a symbol but does not have physical attributes. By definition, there is nothing before Yhwh (zero or the *unmanifest*).

2. You shall not worship images.

It is meaningless to worship the *unmanifest*. It also subtly conveyed that one also must not worship the images of rulers, leaders, and organizations in the form of words, pictures, statues, flags, books, and other symbols of power with external authority.

3. You shall not take the name of God in vain.

This commandment discouraged superstitious belief in placating Yhwh with witchcraft, exorcism, and various sacrifices to prevent disease, earthquakes, floods, death, etc. The objective was to move people away from blind faith in rituals to a rational understanding of nature.

4. Remember the Sabbath day, to keep it holy.

The Sabbath is meant to provide rest amidst efforts devoted to existential needs. Our biological cycles are probably tied to the ocean whose ebbs and tides are related to the phases of the moon. The monthly menstrual cycle of women, e.g., closely follows the lunar cycle. Hindus fast on the eleventh day (*Ekadashi*) from the full moon and the new moon. Celebration of the Sabbath reinvigorates internal energy and lets us lead an enthusiastic life.

5. Honor your father and your mother.

The original commandment probably read, "Love your father and mother." Honor and respect, are social values whereas parents seek a loving relationship. We are unlikely to remember in our conscious minds the unconditional love and care that we received from our parents, especially from our mothers, when we were most vulnerable. Our pain was her pain, and our joy was her joy. In fact, we were an integral part of our mother in her womb. By loving our parents, we imbibe the qualities of empathy and compassion that are essential for a healthy mind. It is the same as loving nature for her unconditional gift of life. This commandment creates compassion, empathy, and joy in emotional connection with all forms of life, beginning with parents.

6. You shall not kill.

It means no killing. Period. It fulfills the first principle. This commandment asks us to treat all life with care, including animals. People have disingenuously differentiated between killing and murder. Voltaire observed (Redman 1949): "It is forbidden to kill; therefore, all murderers are punished unless they kill in large numbers and to the sound of trumpets."

7. You shall not commit adultery.

It also refers to the fulfillment of the first principle. Adultery involves deception. While passion is induced by carnal desires, this precept suggests the need for concern for the feelings of the affected individuals. It asks us not to do to others, what we would not like them to do to us. It asks us to build relationships based on trust, mutual care, and love. Such an approach would not only help us individually but liberate the entire society from its hypocritical ways.

8. You shall not steal.

It also asks for the fulfillment of the first principle. Stealing is an admission of avarice. Human beings are endowed with a generous heart, but an impoverished mind converts them into thieves. Not to steal is not a moral injunction but an entreaty to focus on being self-reliant and realize that thievery causes fear in oneself and pain in others.

Organized religions have treated stealing as a crime and have helped rulers make it a part of the legal system to punish those who violate it, but the rulers themselves have been exempt from stealing and punishment. The perpetrators of massive thefts are not called thieves or robbers but eulogized as kings, emperors, and great conquerors. Colonization and theft of lands, minerals, and properties in Africa, America, Asia, Australia, and Europe through violent means and deception could not have taken place without violating this commandment.

9. You shall not bear false witness against your neighbor.

We are being asked to refrain from telling lies and deceiving others to derive personal benefits. Telling lies is a tacit admission of an inferior life of fetter and fear. Being authentic is the first and last step to freedom. It promotes conscious living with awareness. It encourages healthy and trusting relationships and prevents breach of contract and promises. This commandment also emphasizes the need for fulfilling the first principle.

10. You shall not covet.

The tenth commandment consolidates the last four injunctions. People will naturally become fearless, peaceful, creative, and loving without coveting. It is impossible to kill, deceive, steal, tell lies, or commit adultery when one does not covet.

Summary

Regardless of whether we are religious or non-religious, the diligent practice of the Ten Commandments will lead to self-awareness and liberation.

The Five Yama and Five Niyama of Yoga

The first principle has taken different forms in the East. Zarathustra taught the need for practicing good thoughts (*humata*), good words (*hukhta*), and good deeds (*huvarshta*). Hinduism, Buddhism, and Jainism also have precepts similar to the Ten Commandments. The Buddha referred to it as *sila*. Kongzi introduced the *principle* in China.

Patanjali's *Yoga Sutra* describes five *yama* and five *niyama* as a preventive measure for both physical and mental health, as described below.

The Five Yama of Yoga

All the five yama of yoga are devoted to the implementation of the first principle.

1. Ahimsa (non-violence): Do no harm to anyone in words, deeds or spirit.

It is more encompassing than the sixth commandment, "Don't kill." It refers to the practice of non-violence not only in relation to human beings but also with respect to animals. Do not harm them. Protect them and take care of them. Nature will return the kindness a million-fold. Practicing this precept will make us understand others better. It eliminates negative emotions like fear and guilt and allows us to relate to everyone with empathy and friendliness.

2. Satya (Truth): Adherence to the truth. It is the counterpart of the ninth commandment.

This precept is based on a simple observation: it is falsehood that has corrupted the mind and caused all the suffering. The best antidote to falsehood is truth. Ultimately, it is the truth that liberates. It is best to adhere to truth from the get-go. Nature strictly adheres to truth. Hence, falsehood is opposed to nature. Anything we do that opposes our innate nature will cause pain and suffering. Self-awareness and liberation emerge from the truth.

Ahimsa and Satya were used to great effect by Mahatma Gandhi in his freedom struggle. He reinforced Ahimsa with the truth and called it *Satyagraha* or true non-violent struggle.

3. Asteya (non-stealing): It is exactly the same as the eighth commandment.

In one stroke, this precept clears up a big chunk of space in the mind and keeps it empty forever. It prevents jealousy and greed. It will lead to a world without police and military forces.

The Buddhist philosopher and monk Nagarjuna guided a thief away from thievery in a subtle manner, as described in the following anecdote.

A queen, an admirer of Nagarjuna, invited him to her palace for a meal. As he was about to leave at the end of the meal, she offered to replace his old wooden begging bowl with a golden bowl studded with precious gems and sought to keep the wooden begging bowl for herself as a memento, half hoping that he would reject the offer. However, Nagarjuna accepted it, as gold or wood made no difference to him.

Later, as he left the palace with the precious bowl, a thief eagerly followed him. Nagarjuna entered a deserted temple to take rest, while the thief waited outside for an opportune moment to steal the bowl. Nagarjuna, who was aware of being followed, lobbed the bowl toward the thief who was hiding behind the wall. The thief was flabbergasted. He could not believe that anyone could throw away such a precious object.

Driven by curiosity, the thief wanted to know what it would take anyone to treat treasure with such indifference. He came in, prostrated, and asked Nagarjuna if it was possible for a thief like himself to achieve such a state. Nagarjuna answered in the affirmative. When the thief sought specific instructions, Nagarjuna asked him to continue his practice of stealing with one difference: always remain completely aware of what he was doing. He asked the thief to meet him again in a couple of weeks for further instructions.

Wondering how it could make any difference if he continued to steal, the thief decided to follow the instructions anyway. The next time he went to burgle a house, he suddenly remembered the instructions to be aware of what he was doing. He reflected on how his action was going to adversely affect the family and children as a result of losing their wealth. He decided that it would not be fair to them. He had his own family and children whom he loved. He returned home empty-handed, without stealing. The same thing happened the following night, and the next. Finally, he realized that Nagarjuna had tricked him, as he could not steal anymore!

He went back to Nagarjuna, became a disciple, and was eventually enlightened.

4. Brahmacharya: It is the counterpart of the seventh commandment, viz., injunction against adultery. It is often (incorrectly) identified with chastity.

Brahmacharya means maintaining focus on the true nature of Brahma or Creation. It has little to do with the distorted religious views of celibacy and sinful nature of sex. In ancient times, those who practiced yoga under the guidance of a teacher were usually children, who were playfully absorbed in nature. One needs to be like a child to be free, just as Jesus observed.

This precept is misunderstood to mean that we should remain celibate. Such an interpretation is incorrect. The teachers themselves were not celibate. India was liberal and explicit sex was carved in temples. Goddesses are worshiped as the source of energy (*Kali*), wealth (*Laxmi*), and knowledge (*Saraswathi*). Some of the societies were matriarchal. This precept must be viewed as a need to focus on one's own innate nature (Brahma) and living in accordance with it.

5. Aparigraha (don't covet): It is exactly the same as the tenth commandment.

The Five Niyama of Yoga

The Five niyama of yoga focus on preventing harm to physical and mental wellbeing.

1. Shaucha (Hygiene): Shaucha means cleanliness or hygiene, which protects the body from disease-causing germs. Over three millennia ago, Vedic Rishis gave cleanliness the highest importance for physical wellbeing. The *Yoga Sutra* insists that the body must be clean and in good health to realize liberation.

2. Santosha (contentment): Santosha is being grateful for whatever nature has given. Muhammad referred to contentment as gratitude or thankfulness (*shukriya*). Santosha is emotional fulfillment that is possible only in the absence of greed and envy that cause suffering (*dukkha*). Contentment prevents fear and anxiety. Contentment is a strong emotional need for every individual. Yoga Sutras are ultimately focused on fulfilling emotional needs.

3. Tapasya (austerity): The conventional meaning of *tapasya* is austerity, but its real purpose is to generate internal energy in a disciplined manner by minimizing waste, e.g., by preventing dissipation in debilitating or frivolous thoughts and deeds. It is meant to use all the available energy from digested food for understanding the true nature of the body and the mind. Benefits accrue naturally. It is related to the observance of the Sabbath as well as other disciplines like fasting and prayers that create internal energy and prevent indolence.

4. Svadhyaya: Learning to be self-disciplined and independent of external authority. Being self-taught is the only way to know ourselves.

5. Ishvarapranidhana (understanding *Ishvara*): Become aware of the nature of Ishvara, which is another name for reality, without dissipating energy in image worship. This precept is the same as the first and second commandments, which relate to the trinity. This niyama, like the first two commandments, is asking the individual to understand the nature of reality.

Summary

It is more than a mere coincidence that almost identical secular precepts are described in every major religion. It is the foundation on which the path to liberation is paved. They are not opposed to anyone, any group, or tribe, but focused only on the individual. Implementation of the precepts is vital for the realization of mental freedom. *It must be reiterated that morals, sin, and punishment are not mentioned in the Ten Commandments or yama and niyama.*

Practicing the first principle will certainly prevent mental disturbances from taking root in the mind, but it will do little to what already exists in the mind.

The next chapter is devoted to the **exploration** of the body-emotion-mind coupling to identify, understand, and mitigate mental disturbances.

7

Exploration

Explore with your heart.
—**Kongzi** *(Confucius 1995)*

Exploration focuses on understanding the nature of ignorance that allows us to willingly receive, embrace, and act on ideas that eventually cause mental suffering.

Just as hygiene, balanced diet, and physical exercise are necessary but not sufficient to maintain physical health (as one could get infected with disease), diligent practice of the first principle, '*do not do to others what we would not like others to do to us,*' is necessary but not sufficient for maintaining a healthy mind. We could be mentally conditioned to receive and act on ideas that eventually cause suffering. We lack scientific diagnostic tools to identify the cause of suffering because, unlike physical diseases, mental suffering is abstract, unique to an individual, and the contents of the mind are inaccessible to external agents and tools.

On the other hand, nature has given us unique access to our minds. Unlike the body that is vulnerable to infections through external sources, e.g., pathogens, over which we may have little control, our mind cannot be violated without our cooperation. Thus, the ultimate responsibility for our mental wellbeing rests with us. It is an in-built advantage that we could use wisely to conduct self-inquiry or **exploration** of the mind to identify the weaknesses that allow the voluntary infliction of suffering on ourselves.

Exploration of the mind requires a healthy body and a calm environment to let one meditate for hours without being disturbed. This chapter describes

Patanjali's eight-fold yoga aphorism, *Ashtanga Yoga Sutra*, which is ideally suited for the **exploration** of the mind. All the essential details, including the meaning and purpose of each step, are given. It is an exciting adventure into one's own mind, but it needs discipline to practice it regularly as it may take a while to recognize and clear the mind of all its current disturbances.

Exploration of your own mind will expose mistakes committed in the past. It may be a miserable experience to recall them, but it could be cathartic. You will eventually realize that the past is past; dead and gone. You cannot reconstruct it. The present is yours. It is a precious present from nature to be used wisely. Once you are through with **exploration**, life is never the same again. Life becomes a wonderful adventure.

It would be useful to create a *logbook* of major sources of mental disturbances and prioritize them in terms of intensity and urgency. Even if it takes more effort, it may be best to begin with the heavyweights first. It will eliminate a major source of fear and anxiety and the progress will be rapid once you have figured out how to deal with them.

Patanjali's Ashtanga Yoga Sutra

Patanjali's *Ashtanga Yoga Sutra* is secular, rational, and independent of external authority. Hence, Krishna referred to it as Raja Yoga or the Royal Path to liberation.

Patanjali defined yoga as *chitta vritti nirodhah* (eradication of mental disturbances). That's it. As Hillel might say, the rest is details!

The eight-fold yoga consists of:

1. *Yama:* Precepts for the mind
2. *Niyama:* Discipline for the body and mind
3. *Asanas:* Popularly known simply as yoga or physical postures
4. *Pranayama:* breathing exercise
5. *Pratyahara:* Introspection
6. *Dharana:* External Focus
7. *Dhyana:* Meditation
8. *Samadhi:* Harmony and Mental Balance

The goal of yoga is the elimination of mental disturbances with harmonious functioning of feelings, *thoughts, words, and actions* to fulfill innate emotional needs.

Yama and niyama were discussed in Phase I on **prevention**. Yoga continues with the development of a supple body and efforts to recognize the connection between body and emotion and between emotion and mind in the next five steps to intuitively realize samadhi or mental balance at the eighth.

We begin **exploration** with asanas for physical conditioning.

3. Asanas or Hatha Yoga

Yoga has become synonymous with hatha yoga or *asanas*. Yoga classes have sprouted everywhere. The medical field has begun to recognize the positive health benefits of yoga. However, it may be of interest to note that only one verse out of a total of about 200 verses in *Ashtanga Yoga Sutra* is devoted to the popular form of yoga. Patanjali stated: be seated comfortably (*sthirasukham aasanam*). That's it. The popular yoga manual with hundreds of postures is merely a preparation for *Debugging the Mind*. Be seated comfortably!

As we are aware, astronauts undergo thorough physical conditioning in preparation for the rigors of outer-space exploration that imposes extreme demands on both the body and the mind. Apart from withstanding the tremendous physical stresses that such a journey imposes on the body, a well-conditioned body is also necessary to let the astronauts remain alert and focused on the challenges posed by the risk-laden adventure.

Asanas serve a similar purpose for inner-space **exploration**. Obviously, the demands imposed on the body and mind are different from outer-space exploration as we usually do not face life-threatening situations during meditation, but one needs to remain sensitive to the subtlest thoughts and emotions that arise in the mind, which are easy to miss with an ill-conditioned body. Meditating and remaining alert for hours requires a good physical condition. The purpose of asanas is to be able to sit comfortably and meditate for hours.

Asanas take care of every muscle, every joint, every ligament, every cartilage, every sinew, and practically every part of the body to make it a smooth and well-lubricated machine, in which all components are naturally aligned to perform optimally with the least dissipation of energy. The primary goal is to keep the body healthy and supple so that it allows the mind to remain focused on self-inquiry for hours without physical distractions.

4. Pranayama: Body-Emotion Coupling

Pranayama is focused on understanding the body-emotion connection.

Prana refers to the breath (life-source or energy) that sustains life. We breathe in oxygen to create energy by burning internal fuel, and we breathe out the unwanted by-products. Prana is subtly related to emotions. We can recognize the connection between our breathing (prana) and emotions, e.g., when we are angry, excited, fearful, etc. When we cry or laugh, breathing becomes hard. When we are in awe or in love, we may forget to breathe with a dropped jaw and a gaping mouth! Our breathing is shallow and erratic when our mind is restless and anxious. Our breathing is regular and deep when our mind is calm.

Pranayama is a practical technique learned from babies. Healthy babies have supple bodies and breathe with a natural rhythm. One could observe how rhythmically they breathe in peaceful sleep. When a baby is awake, it is fully awake. When it is playful, it is lost in playfulness. It knows how to get help from nature. Its screams are full-throated and get the necessary attention. When it is relaxed, it is completely relaxed, it sleeps with no concern for the future. Babies are the original yoga masters.

It is possible to reverse the process and use breath as a feedback signal to monitor our emotions. When anger begins to surface, e.g., we could focus on breathing deeply and we will notice that anger subsides on its own. Anxiety is reduced when we breathe deeply.

We get many opportunities in our human interactions when anxiety and mental stress levels tend to go up. We generally tend to react to them unconsciously. We must practice pranayama in real-time when we face those situations. Keep anger, hatred, etc. on temporary hold. Take deep breaths. Don't build more negative thoughts. Continue to take deep breaths until you begin to realize a significant drop in your pulse rate. Pranayama is beneficial for the heart as well as the mind.

Gurdjieff, the well-known spiritual leader mentions in one of his books the great advice he received from his father just before he passed away. His father asked him to do nothing for twenty-hours when he was angry. It is likely that during that period both the intensity of anger and its relevance would disappear.

The purpose of pranayama is to pay close attention to emotions, as the intellect is usually focused on logic, reason, and justifications. Nobody knows the source of emotion. An identical trigger could evoke completely differ-ent responses from different individuals. A healthy individual might roll with laughter, but a high-strung person might pull the trigger and watch the other roll dead or inflict damage on oneself. Emotions arise first and the intellect follows later with a finite time-delay. This time-delay could act to stabilize or destabilize the mind. The purpose of pranayama is to use this time-delay to better understand the nature of emotions that trigger a response.

Pranayama is a passive control of emotions through silent observation. It reveals the nature of disturbances that arise in the mind.

5. Pratyahara: Introspection

Pratyahara explores the mind-emotion connection.

Pratyahara is carried out to understand the nature of internal desires and how they affect us. Pratyahara literally means "without food intake" (no food for thought). Just as we allow the stomach to digest the food that is consumed before eating again, we need to let the mind digest existing thoughts and emo-tions. It is introspection.

Our lives seem to be a continuous struggle to satisfy our cravings that motivate us to act either one way or the other. The intellect offers reasons to act in a particular manner based on knowledge and past experiences. We usu-ally await the outcome with bated breath, fear, anxiety, or excitement.

Mental disturbances arise when we feel threatened. We may perceive threats to what we are seeking: material gain, social status, and other desires. Our mental disturbances are directly related to our desire or craving. We feel upset when we perceive anyone doing anything to prevent us from achieving it.

All our sense organs are designed to probe external inputs. Eyes cannot see within, ears cannot listen to themselves, a nose cannot smell itself, a tongue cannot taste itself, and so on. In stark contrast, however, the mind is capable of probing its own thoughts.

In pratyahara, the sense organs are deliberately prevented from seeking exter-nal objects to allow the mind to look at itself without external distractions. It is a crucial stage of the journey when the mind is thoroughly probed in long spells of silent meditation. It is a time to review the challenges posed by the practice of the first principle. It is a time to verify if the known feelings, thoughts, words, and actions are aligned with the emotions. And, how cravings affect them.

It is a time to identify the source of the problem with the highest priority as listed in the logbook. The mind is encouraged to return to the problem when it tries to wander away and cling to thoughts that involve external objects and values, resentments and approval, likes and dislikes, etc. We must find a solution that completely eliminates the problem without harming anyone in the process. Practicing the first principle will prevent new additions to the list. This process must be continued until all the items in the logbook are eliminated.

A Thought Experiment (Gdanken)

To better understand pratyahara, you could conduct a thought experiment in which you are all by yourself in the entire universe, where there is no one to deceive and nothing to receive, no predator and no prey, and no birth and no death. How would you think and act in such a world?

How would you determine what is right and wrong, good and evil? Do lying, cheating, stealing, killing, and adultery mean anything in the absence of the other? It becomes clear that they acquire meaning only with the emergence of the images of the other in the mind. All interactions, including love and conflicts, take place between your self-image and the images of the other in your mind. Your dualistic ideas of friends and enemies, love and hatred, revenge and forgiveness, praises and condemnations, promises and deceits, war and peace, etc. are transactions between these images and your self-image.

You may have all the images of the external world in your mind but essentially you are still all by yourself, alone in this vast universe. Wouldn't this reveal that, when you are all by yourself, deception would be tantamount to self-deception? And aren't emotions like fear, anxiety, and insecurity created by the images of the self and others?

The above *gdanken* experiment is not a frivolous fantasy. When you deeply introspect, you will realize that it is, in fact, reality that appears and disappears like sweet dreams or nightmares. They appear real when we are awake and even during dreams and nightmares. They disappear altogether when we are in deep sleep.

Zhuangzi once posed the following teaser: he said, "I dreamed last night that I was a butterfly but now I am not sure whether it was me who had the dream of being a butterfly or it is the butterfly that is now dreaming that it is Zhuangzi. Which is real?"

The entire drama is being played on a screen in the brain and we get identified with the main character of the drama, who also happens to be the producer, scriptwriter, director, and the entire audience. Our conditioned minds enact the ultimate comedy (or tragedy) of errors when we assume the images to be real.

It is relatively easy to simulate the scenario of being alone in a monastic setting. For example, in the Zen monastery at Sogenji, we could even have the luxury of living in isolation in a small cabin at the mountaintop where we could spend a whole week all alone. Solitary confinement is usually considered a severe punishment in a prison, but in this monastery, it is a much sought-after privilege with a waiting list. During that week, it is impossible to violate any of the precepts, because we are all alone and will not be encountering another person. It allows the individual to realistically conduct the above gdanken experiment, which is the essence of pratyahara.

Eventually, pratyahara will enable us to digest and eliminate major mental disturbances and will reveal the innermost emotions that are as important to the mind as food, water, and air are for the body. They are the true source of inspiration and passion in life, that provide the energy for our actions. When they are aligned with our innate nature, we will not experience any hindrance and we will naturally feel fulfilled.

Recollections of the past may lead to uncontrollable sobbing, which could be cathartic.

6. Dharana: External Focus or Concentration

Having learned in *pratyahara* to digest internal thoughts and feelings without new external inputs, the mind is now allowed to move outward. The mind tends to wander and become restless. To avoid this restlessness, we practice *dharana*, (focus or concentration). It is meant to train the mind to focus on a single object, regardless of how trivial or important it is. It may be the tip of our nose or a small candlelit flame in front of us.

We need to bring the body to cooperate with the mind to do dharana. It is not as easy or trivial as it might sound. Followers of the Soto lineage do zazen facing a blank wall. In Zen monasteries of the Rinzai tradition, where I went, a monk (or nun) walks up and down the aisle to make sure that you sit still. Any physical movement indicating a loss of focus is met with four sharp blows on the shoulder with a flat cane to bring you back to the present.

When I did zazen at Sogenji, I sat facing a wall. The aisle was between me and the wall. Right behind me was an open window, which allowed cold breeze into the hall and froze me during autumn months. The big hall where higher ups in the totem pole sat, there were two platforms facing each other, but separated by a big open space.

The practice of *dharana*, or focusing on an external object, allows us to recognize how restless our minds are and how difficult it is to bring them back to the present. Practically all the wandering of the mind could be traced to intellectual pursuits to satisfy our cravings. The wandering mind remains focused only when intellectualization stops, as logic and reason play no role in simply focusing on an object. It is only when we have the desire to do something with an object that the intellect jumps in with its clever schemes.

A focused mind learns to differentiate between actions that are driven by reason and those by innate emotions. Practically all actions where reason plays the primary role, can be traced to external objects of desire. Actions based on innate emotions, on the other hand, are self-driven, with reason playing a secondary, but supportive role.

7. Dhyana: Meditation or Zen

The last stage of **exploration** is to let the mind move freely in an unconstrained manner. *Dhyana* outwardly resembles both pratyahara and dharana, but it is fundamentally different from both. In all three stages, one can observe the practitioner sitting silently like a statue, but there the similarity ends. In dhyana, there is no concentration, no focus, and no clinging to thoughts or sensory inputs.

Dhyana is complete relaxation; pure and passive observation. The mind is allowed complete freedom to find natural alignment with the surrounding energy field. The mind is unleashed, to let the individual become aware of its activities as an unbiased observer. It is as if one is in deep sleep and yet completely awake. It prepares the individual for the final state of *samadhi* or mental balance. It is already trained not to cling to sense-oriented objects in pratyahara and to stay focused and alert in dharana. The mind is allowed to watch itself in dhyana without interference from the sense organs or judgment. The individual becomes a pure observer of the body, mind, and emotions.

8. *Samadhi* or Mental Balance

Patanjali assumed that *samadhi* would be naturally realized at the end of the seventh step, but it remains a distant dream for most people. Some people develop physical skills through the practice of *hatha yoga* and become professional teachers of yoga (*asanas*). Others, who have realized a relatively calm mind, become teachers of meditative practices. However, samadhi cannot be realized with more of the same. One must recognize the underlying causes of mental disturbances and completely eliminate them to realize samadhi.

Although *Ashtanga Yoga Sutra* takes one through physical exercises and thought processes, Patanjali himself defined the aim of yoga as *chitta vritti nirodhah*: elimination of mental disturbances, and not as any kind of physical or intellectual accomplishment. The first seven steps of Yoga were to prevent the body and intellect from being an impediment to mental wellbeing. *Mental disturbances are caused by emotional discontent and not because of intellectual deficit.*

The inability to realize samadhi is primarily caused by the false perception that it requires a high degree of mental concentration. Many authors have incorrectly translated dhyana as concentration and samadhi (nirvana) as perfect concentration, but the very strenuous effort to concentrate and attain an exalted mental state would cause mental disturbances. It is hard to acquire even physical skills like swimming or riding a bicycle when the body is stiff or in a panic mode. What facilitates the realization of samadhi (nirvana) is not concentration but the very opposite: *relaxation*. Be completely at ease.

Remarkable figures like the Buddha, Jesus, and Socrates were not intellectual geniuses but emotionally contented and peaceful people. In stark contrast, brilliant thinkers like Pascal and Nietzsche were intellectual giants but emotionally discontented and restless men.

Samadhi is complete emotional contentment and not an intellectual realization. Hence, traditional efforts based on dualistic logic and reason have failed. The final chapter on **Experimentation** describes practices that create the intuition that is required to realize the mental harmony to lead a balanced life.

8

Experimentation

When parents preach what they do not practice,
children learn what they are not taught.

The final chapter of *Debugging the Mind* is devoted to the realization of mental harmony regardless of the external factors. It is based on systematically strengthening our relatively weaker cognitive functions through practical **experimentation**, thereby eliminating internal discord that causes fear, anxiety, and insecurity. *Debugging the Mind* is naturally complete when the discord is eliminated, and internal harmony is restored.

In Chapter 3, Krishna described four paths to the realization of liberation (Fosse 2007) based on the four cognitive functions *sensing, feelings, thinking, and intuition.*

For those with reasonably well-balanced sensing, feeling, and thinking functions, and a strong intuition, Patanjali's *Ashtanga Yoga Sutra* is sufficient to give that little extra push to attain complete balance. **Exploration** of the body-mind-emotion system will enable the practitioner to intuitively realize mental balance and samadhi.

Of the remaining three, viz., sensing, feeling, and thinking, progress in science and technology has greatly reduced our dependence on physical strength, as machines do most of the hard work. People merely operate these machines, which, for the most part, requires only technical expertise, and not muscular power. Thus, unlike what it used to be in ancient times, weakness in sensing function does not cause huge emotional imbalance today.

The primary source of imbalance in the world today is caused by the huge gap between thinking and feeling functions. We have put logic and reason on a pedestal and ignored emotions. Disingenuous use of logic and reason were made to justify slavery, subjugation of women, and slaughter of millions in the name of king, god, race, ethnicity, ideology, etc. Even today, logical justifications based on knowledge and power are used to hurt, deceive, exploit, and control people. As Einstein observed, "We cannot solve our problems with the same thinking we used when we created them."

The Buddha, Jesus, and Muhammad developed methods that are well suited for eradicating artificially created biases, boundaries, and animosities. Their approaches are most relevant today because *we are suffering from surplus thinking and deficit feeling.*

The Buddha, Jesus, and Muhammad—The Masters

The Buddha, Jesus, and Muhammad were gentle, emotionally secure, and peaceful men. They developed three distinct paths that are tailored to meet the needs of individuals with thinking, feeling, and sensing as dominant cognitive functions. They used paradoxical, implicit, and subtle techniques to strengthen the weaker functions.

The Buddha's approach focused on strengthening the feeling and sensing functions of intellectuals. Jesus focused on strengthening the thinking and sensing functions of feelers. Muhammad focused on inculcating thinking and feeling functions in sensors. All the three focused on creating inner harmony, which was referred to as *nirvana* by the Buddha, liberation by Jesus, and *Islam* or peace by Muhammad. How their paradoxical approaches guide us to realize nirvana, liberation, or peace is described in the following sections.

The interpretation of their lives and teachings throughout the book reflects my understanding. Events described are fictional. My love and admiration for them let me treat them as friends and loved ones. No disrespect is intended to anyone.

The Buddha in Bodh Gaya

The Gaps

Dualistic interpretations have caused many gaps in understanding the Buddha's teachings. We briefly look at some of them. For example, the Buddha asserted that ignorance was the cause of suffering and introduced an eight-fold Noble Path to end suffering and realize *nirvana*, but we lack a uniformly valid and unique definition of both 'ignorance' and 'nirvana'.

The eight-fold Noble Path is usually (and imprecisely) translated as right attitude (*Samma-Ditthi*), right thought (*Samma-Sankappa*), right speech (*Samma-Vaca*), right action (*Samma Kammanta*), right occupation (*Samma-Ajiva*), right effort (*Samma-Vayama*), right mindfulness (*Samma-Sati*), and right concentration (*Samma-Samadhi*).

The eight-fold path as stated above cannot be uniquely described without defining the word 'right.' In the absence of a uniformly valid and invariant frame of reference for right and wrong values, these statements do not have unique logical meaning. As described later in this section, the word 'right' must be replaced by the word 'balanced' to indicate a stable mind with zero mental disturbances at each stage.

In practice, all these concepts have been logically interpreted without a uniformly valid and invariant definition of what is right and what is wrong. Even *nirvana* has been falsely interpreted as right concentration, which implies an object of focus. It is unlikely that the Buddha meant it that way. Such translations are made by people who look at nirvana as an intellectual accomplishment. If anything, *nirvana* is the very lack of concentration. It is a state of let-go, complete relaxation, and being naturally alert, like a cat. Everything gets done in accordance with the eternal principle (*dhamma*). The Zen masters, who intuitively realized it, gave lusty blows to discourage disciples from indulging in discursive logic. They also introduced *koans* that defy logic.

The Buddha's approach involves becoming a mendicant, which sounds dismal. Our social status will go into a tailspin if we became a beggar. The very idea of begging for freedom sounds like an oxymoron. Intellectuals tend to view ignorance as a lack of knowledge and expect to realize nirvana just like they acquire expertise in physics or mathematics. It is difficult to realize that the path to nirvana is through mendicancy.

The Buddha was keenly aware that the gap between his teachings and the realization of nirvana cannot be logically bridged. He is known to have gently persuaded intellectuals to move away from dualistic logic to a direct understanding of the nature of the self through diligent practice of his teachings, as exemplified by the following incident in his life.

A brilliant scholar, who himself had thousands of followers, approached the Buddha, and asked him to describe nirvana, adding that he was well versed in logic and scriptures, and that he was earnest and willing to listen to him. The Buddha agreed to do so on one condition: the scholar had to stay in the sangha for one year, follow instructions, silently observe every small detail of his life without asking any questions, and at the end of one year he'd receive the answer. When Buddha said this, the assembled monks heard loud laughter from a senior disciple, who rarely spoke or laughed. Surprised at his explosive laughter, the assembled disciples asked him to explain.

Addressing the scholar, he said, "Don't listen to the Buddha. I came to him with the same question a few years ago and he responded the same way. I stayed with him for a year and followed his instructions, silently observing every aspect of his life and mine. At the end of the year, I was left with no more questions! They vanished. If you really want to get a logical answer, insist on getting it now, when you are still ignorant. Next year, I warn you, you'll have no more questions left. The Buddha is tricky!"

Even his loving disciple called him a trickster without a trace of fear or condemnation, which is an amazing and amusing compliment.

The contents of the mind have to come to a boiling point of contradictions to evaporate and vanish altogether, revealing the absolute truth. Instead of offering a dry form of logic, the Buddha took the intellectuals in the exact opposite direction, toward humility, empathy, and compassion by making them mendicants. Apart from making them humble, it exposed them to the kindness of people who generously gave them alms without any expectations in return. In the process, empathy and compassion slowly took root within them.

The path to *nirvana* is not through the intellect and dualistic logic, but through the heart; through diligent practice and **experimentation**.

The Life and Message of the Buddha

The Buddha spent nearly four decades preaching a god-less religion. He rejected all prevailing religions and their gods, but nobody killed him. On the other hand, kings as well as ordinary people felt safe and peaceful around him. Wealthy people donated land for him and his disciples to live and practice their way of life. Scholars thronged to hear him, debate with him, and many became his disciples. He covered a vast territory in India by foot and reached out to people. Later, people from China and the Far-East visited India to learn more about his teachings, which naturally spread throughout the world without shedding blood.

The Buddha did not speculate on esoteric concepts and strongly discouraged dualistic interpretations of his own teachings. His approach appeals to intellectuals, as his teachings are rational, secular, and practical. He was focused on reducing mental disturbances to zero (shunya). He referred to the self as anatta or no-self and the nature of reality as shunyata or emptiness. The Buddha described a paradoxical approach to realize it.

The *Buddha's approach is relevant for those whose dominant cognitive function is thinking.* Their *sensing* and *feeling* functions tend to be relatively weak. Intellectuals also tend to be conceited. I know! The Buddha addressed these weaknesses in his teachings.

I asked the Buddha how he realized nirvana.

"I faced a dilemma in my personal life," the Buddha admitted, "which I tried to solve with an intellect that was a dwarf compared to that of giants like Newton and Einstein. I did not have the faintest idea of nirvana. I was more concerned about mundane matters such as the presence of sorrow (*dukkha*) in my life and in the lives of people I loved. Suffering seemed to be a universal phenomenon, whereas everyone desired happiness (*sukha*). People lived with fear, anxiety and insecurity all through their lives. Being a prince, I also knew that even the king was prone to these debilitating emotions. Everyone faced the possibility of infirmity at old age, painful disease, loss of loved ones, and death. I wanted to know how to lead a free, fearless, and fulfilling life despite these ominous threats.

"Religious texts mention that after a long practice lasting many years in the forest, I suddenly achieved nirvana just before dawn as the planet Venus rose in the sky. They do not describe what triggered this remarkable transformation. I shall describe the event now."

"As you know," the Buddha continued "I left the pleasures of my kingdom and entered the forest to live with ascetics to find a solution to end mental suffering. Since they appeared to be content with an austere life in the forest in spite of all its hardships, I thought that they might have the answers. For a prince used to the luxuries of life in a palace with many attendants eager to take care of my physical needs, it was not an easy transition.

"For many years, I diligently practiced every task that I was assigned. I practiced yoga, chanted prayers, meditated, and did everything, including hard labor and keeping the environment clean. I fulfilled the first principle and even became a vegetarian as a part of my vow not to harm any life. I led an austere life to check the limits of my endurance, became physically weak and famished, and came to a point where I was stuck with a future that was empty and meaningless. I was close to being totally disillusioned with the effort. The folks who were trying to guide me also seemed to be stuck at the same point for years, no closer to the end of suffering. Having reached a point of no return, they appeared stoic.

"I now faced the ultimate dilemma: either there is a solution or there is no solution. It was clear that no one was going to hand the solution to me on a platter. It was like the blind guiding the blind. I had to figure it out independently. I had no choice. I knew that there was no way back, as conventional life too was meaningless. I was at a dead-end. It appeared as if all my efforts were in vain. Instead of ending suffering, I was acutely experiencing it. I sat under a fig tree and contemplated for days on end with no result. I became so weak and emaciated that I could hardly get up and walk to find food. It was a hot day in May.

"Then the inexplicable happened.

"A young girl, Sujata, came and offered a bowl of rice sweetened with milk and honey. She looked so happy to offer it with no expectations other than to feed my hunger. She looked so contented. The very giving to a needy person seemed to make her immensely happy. It suddenly dawned on me that this caring, compassionate, and unconditional giving attitude was what I had been missing all my life.

"As a prince, I was well trained in logic and reason (*thinking*), and well versed in martial arts (*sensing*), but *feeling* was the weakest link in my selfish mind. Until then, I was merely concerned with my suffering and how to end it. She made me realize that my suffering would naturally disappear when I cared for others. *Sujata was my real guru.*

"There was a palpable end to all the tension in my mind. I felt so peaceful. With utmost gratitude, I ate her offerings, and went to sleep like a baby.

"When I awoke the next morning and saw the bright planet Venus effortlessly rise in the sky, I realized that it had been doing it before I was born and likely to continue after I am gone. I saw spontaneity in all aspects of nature, whereas my suffering was self-inflicted by clinging to selfish cravings and expectations. I felt relieved of a huge burden when my clinging to self-image ceased, the resistance vanished, and I suddenly felt extraordinarily peaceful. It was a simple truth, but I had taken a circuitous route to get there.

"Of course, it may appear that if I were to do it all over again, I would cut out some extraneous rituals and random walks, but I saw the vital role played by every small step that I had taken, however meaningless it might have been. They created the right amount of tension in the mind and made it finely tuned and sensitive. One timely and kind gesture from Sujata snapped it and made it vanish without a trace. I recognized that a logical path to this realization did not exist. What is possible is to let you reach this tipping-point of contradictions in a logical manner and leave you there to fend for yourself!

"It may appear callous, but it happens to be the most effective approach. It is like teaching a child to swim by letting her in a swimming pool, providing initial support as needed. and then letting go. It is the same as what a mother does when she teaches her baby to walk. I am absolutely certain that if you were to diligently follow the three-phase approach of *Debugging the Mind*, you would eventually be liberated. Your attitude plays the most critical role, as described in the following anecdote.

"An old man and a young man were conducting severe penance. After many years of penance, God appeared in front of the old man and asked him what he was seeking. The old man said that he wanted to know when he would be liberated. God told him that it would take the old man as many reincarnations as the number of leaves on the fig tree under which he was sitting. Being aware that there were thousands of leaves on that tree, the old man became discouraged and gave up. God then went to the young man who also asked the same question and received the same answer. The young man jumped in joy and exclaimed, 'Awesome, so one day I too will get liberated, Cool!' and instantly became liberated.

"I propounded the eight-fold Noble Path to guide you. The contradictions and problems that arise from implementing it in practice, provide the grist for your meditative practices. The transition to nirvana is left unexplained. Dhammapada would take you close to the center and with *diligent practice* you will intuitively bridge the gap.

"This entire process can be divided into four stages," the Buddha continued.

"The first and most crucial step is the arising of the urge to seek liberation. As Shantideva observed, *'The urge for nirvana is as rare as a blind man finding a gem in a heap of rubbish'* (Shantideva 2011). It is up to you to decide whether you want to embark on this journey or stay with your current way of living. Most people seem to prefer the known devil compared to the unknown angel.

"If you find within yourself the courage and commitment to seek liberation, then the second step is the **prevention** of false perceptions of reality from entering your mind. Practicing the first principle, *'do not do to others what you would not want them to do to you,'* will help you realize it.

"Understanding the body-mind-emotion coupling through **exploration** of the mind is the third step. Patanjali described the process in his *Yoga Sutra*.

"The above three steps are practically self-evident and rational. They take you through to the intellectual limits. You could rationally work out the problems and minimize mental disturbances, but a persistent and annoying residue remains. *It is the end of reason.* Now you need a trigger, like what Sujata did to me!

"I introduced the eight-fold Noble Path as the fourth step to create constraints in your life and contradictions in your perception of the true nature of the self. Persistent efforts to maintain *feelings, thoughts, words,* and *actions* in consonance will eventually reveal the innate nature of your mind, create mental harmony, and set you free."

I sought clarifications. "Please explain the true meaning of the teachings."

"I followed a logical path that is known in mathematics *as reductio ad absurdum.* I began with a statement that life is a suffering, but diligent practice of my teachings will show that one could completely eradicate suffering and realize nirvana, which clearly contradicts the first statement," explained the Buddha.

"I divided the process into three parts," he continued.

1. The four Noble Truths that consists of problem statement and assumptions.
2. The eight-fold Noble Path, which is the procedural part with teachings.
3. **Experimentation** to realize nirvana."

The Four Noble Truths

"The four Noble Truths (*Chatvara Arya-satya* or the four-fold Arya-truth) are:

1. Life involves suffering (dukkha or sorrow);
2. It is the result of cravings caused by false perception (ignorance) of reality;
3. It is possible to become aware of the source of ignorance; and
4. It is possible to end suffering by following an eight-fold Noble Path (originally called *Ashtanga Aryamarg* or eight-fold Arya path)."

The Eight-fold Noble Path (*Ashtanga Aryamarg*)

"The word 'Aryan' may have a racist connotation after its abuse by Hitler, but in Sanskrit it refers to the noble quality of people who adhere to the truth. *Marg* means path. The word 'path' could also be misleading because every path has two directions. Just as the word 'right' begs the question, 'what is "wrong?"', the word path leads to the question, which 'direction?' Saying that you must take interstate highway I-95 to go to New York is not sufficient. The same highway could also take you to Miami. You have to specify the direction, I-95N or I-95S depending on where you enter it.

"So, I would like you to interpret *Aryamarg* as a path of truth to nirvana with eight milestones. You could look at the eight-fold Noble Path or eight-fold path of truth as a roadmap with eight important milestones that help ensure that you are headed in the right direction toward nirvana. These milestones, as the word implies, are set in the order in which they must be traversed, with nirvana the desired destination. Remember that it is only a map. You have to do the real traveling to reach the desired destination.

"The path to truth covers the following eight milestones:

1. Balanced View (*Samma-Ditthi*)
2. Balanced Thought (*Samma-Sankappa*)
3. Balanced Word (*Samma-Vaca*)
4. Balanced Action (*Samma-Kammanta*)
5. Balanced Living (*Samma-Ajiva*)
6. Balanced Vocation (*Samma-Vayama*)
7. Balanced Mindfulness (*Samma-Sati*)
8. Complete Balance (*Samma-Samadhi*)

"Every milestone starts with the word 'balanced.' In mathematical terms, these are eight equations that must be simultaneously balanced with a zero (no error) on the right-hand side. In other words, all the milestones must be covered to reach the destination (nirvana). At each step, you must also fulfill both the first and second principles (*Do not do to others what you would not want them to do to you. Maintain feelings, thoughts, words, and actions in harmony*).

"I shall now describe the eight-fold Noble Path."

1. Balanced View (*Samma-Ditthi*)

"*Samma-Ditthi* or Balanced View (Attitude) is a critical milestone. It ensures that you will continue to move toward your center. The opposite direction will take you away from your center. It provides the direction for the rest of the journey. Social conditioning has made you dependent on dualistic values such as rewards and punishment, praise and insults, etc. You may be judging the world to be good or evil, right or wrong, etc.

To end mental suffering, the balanced way to view reality is without judgment; *as it is* and not how *it* ought *to be*. Judging others from your selfish perspective is an impediment to your progress. Some may be moving faster, some may be slow, and some may be going in the opposite direction. Everyone is learning at her/his own pace and ability. Let it be. Nature has her own way to guide people. The origin and the destination are the same for all.

"*The best attitude is to have an attitude of not knowing and learning.* It is the attitude of a person like Socrates. With such an attitude, life is always joyful and enchanting.

2. Balanced Thought (*Samma-Sankappa*)

"Moving further, the first milestone automatically leads to balanced thoughts."

"The second milestone is that of Balanced Thought (*Samma-Sankappa*). A gazillion thoughts are generated to determine the best approach to satisfy the desires for material benefits, social status, praise, awards, etc. that may suggest manipulation, exploitation, and control of others. You might have a wide range of thoughts, from the vilest to the most sublime, but the first principle immediately filters out all those that are harmful to anyone. Balanced attitude helps you maintain the direction to reach the third milestone.

3. Balanced Word (*Samma-Vaca*)

"The third milestone is Balanced Word (*Samma-Vaca*), which is a window to your mind. Usually, your expressions are in response to the inputs from the external world. Unlike thoughts, you have full control over the choice of words that you use to express yourself. Society imposes its own version of control through what is commonly known as being politically correct, polite manners, military orders, etc. Regardless of whether your words are in response to your inner emotions or caused by external stimuli, it is best to keep them balanced: neither harsh nor unctuous. Implementation of the first principle, along with Balanced Attitude and Balanced Thought naturally ensure Balanced Word.

"The third milestone, Balanced Word, is virtually the first stage of **experimentation**. Starting from this step, anything you say or do will have consequences in terms of response or reaction from the external sources. As they could have serious repercussions on your life, I created a safe environment (the sangha) to train people to deal with them at their own pace. This is a critical step in your journey. As there is always a possibility that your words could be misinterpreted with dualistic logic, you will learn to remain steadfast even in the presence of hostile reaction to your well-intentioned expression.

4. Balanced Action (*Samma-Kammanta*)

"It is often difficult to realize the fourth milestone, Balanced Action (*Samma-Kammanta*), when faced with deception, treachery, and violence. It is difficult to determine what is Balanced Action when the dualistic values of society are skewed in favor of the wealthy and powerful who impose their seemingly unfair rules on the rest of society.

"The realization of Balanced Word and Balanced Action poses the greatest problem in practice because they are linked to your desires whose fulfillment often depends on external circumstances. You are generally faced with a dilemma about whether to satisfy the societal values imposed on you or act according to your desires and face the consequences. If you are of the timid type, you tend to let society dictate the terms and if you are of the aggressive type, you tend to impose your will on the rest. In either case, you experience internal conflicts. It is a tough problem whose solution eludes most people. It cannot be solved with dualistic values as long as the real source of emotions remains unknown.

"Although you have little control over your thoughts, you do have the ability to select the one you wish to convert into action. The best way to resolve this problem is to extend the ideas expressed by Zarathustra who taught the need for good thoughts (*humata*), good words (*hukhta*), and good deeds (*huvarshta*), which are the same as Balanced Thought, Balanced Word, and Balanced Action described above.

"Of course, Zarathustra did not define what was good nor did I mention what was balanced because any definition would be only dualistic in nature. What we both meant was identical, intuitive, and absolute. The first principle, *'do not do to others what you would not want them to do to you,'* plays a vital role in the selection of thoughts, words, and actions. You have to be true to yourself however challenging the perceived consequences. It may require a safe environment to practice and better understand the connection between your feelings, thoughts, words, and actions without fear."

At this point, I interjected with, "I have often wondered why most enlightened people, including you, have lived outside of society. Most of us have no desire to live in a forest, an ashram, or be a mendicant. Are we doomed to suffer in society?"

"It is true that most people who have recognized their Buddha-natures have lived apart from society," answered the Buddha. "That list includes me, but it was not because I was afraid or unable to live in society. I found that living apart from society makes it more effective to guide people because I was not perceived as a threat, a competitor, or benefactor of any social assets. The only treasure that I had to offer was the truth.

"Societies in general, and rulers in particular, are afraid of free people, who are perceived to be threats to their selfish desires to subjugate, exploit, and control people. Socrates tried to help people directly as a common man, but he was asked to drink hemlock. Rulers were scared of the gentle presence and free spirit of Jesus; they nailed him to the cross. Muhammad was persecuted.

"On the other hand, when kings themselves are enlightened, people seek petty material gains. Janaka and Krishna were enlightened kings. Muhammad was a businessman who became a ruler. People seek material benefits or power, whereas their infinitely more valuable insights were ignored. Pattinathar, a great 10th-century Tamil poet, was the son of a rich merchant of precious gems. He renounced wealth and became a wandering spiritual leader. He said, "People thronged to buy expensive gems from me. Today, I have freely spread far more precious gems, but there is nary a taker!"

"I decided to remain a mendicant although my father very much wanted me to take care of his kingdom. I wanted to make sure that those who came to me were only interested in seeking their innate nature and not any material benefit that I might have been able to offer as a king. I offered them nothing of material value.

"Although I left my kingdom and my young family, I made sure that their safety and lives were not jeopardized by my absence as they were protected by my father, who was a king. However, it may appear callous on my part to have done so. It was especially cruel to my young wife, who was also dependent on me for fulfilling her emotional needs. My absence also denied my son the presence of a father. You could justifiably blame me.

"Later, I apologized to them for the pain caused by my actions. They forgave me and became my disciples. They were truly kind to me and helped me serve and willingly contributed to what they considered was a greater need for humanity. They too were liberated. Without their implicit support I would not have been able to effectively carry on my work for four decades. To them, I owe immeasurable gratitude.

"I could easily have become a king, as my father wanted, but it would have been practically impossible for me to determine whether people were coming to me for gaining social status, influence, wealth, and power, or with a genuine interest in the teachings. Hence, I stuck to the life of a mendicant. I offered nothing but a verifiable path of truth to nirvana, and that was everything a lover of truth would seek.

"I am not asking you to copy me. It is not necessary. You can be a part of society and still realize nirvana. In fact, I would insist that you remain in society. If you were able to realize nirvana while leading a normal life in the marketplace, then it would be proof that it is possible for everyone. Right now, there is an implicit assumption that one needs to live in a monastery or ashram, wear special robes, and carry out rituals and chanting in order to realize nirvana. It is not true.

"King Janaka was a Buddha. Krishna was a king and a Buddha. Marcus Aurelius, a king, was a Buddha. Socrates, who was a soldier, was a Buddha. Muhammad was a merchant who became a Buddha and ruled Mecca. Vimalakirti, who was a rich businessman during my time and about whom I have often talked, was a Buddha. Jnaneshwar, the kid of Alandi, was a Buddha. Ramana Maharishi whose main message was silence and the cryptic question, "Who am I?" was a Buddha. Ramakrishna, the priest of Kalighat, was a Buddha. Krishnamurthy, who wore suits from Saville Row and raced his car from Los Angeles Airport to his house in Ojai Valley was a Buddha. And so was Nisargadatta who lived in a ghetto in Mumbai, ran a small grocery store, and smoked *bidis* (home-made cigarettes).

"There are many other Buddhas, but you may not be able to recognize them with a dualistic mind. Yes, it is within your capabilities to practice the teachings in the society and realize your Buddha-nature. All human beings can realize their Buddha-natures regardless of their occupations and where they live, because it is their innate nature.

"Your last question is relevant to the modern era. No, you are not doomed to suffer in society. In fact, humanity has made remarkable progress in creating a relatively safe environment. Although it is not as bad as in the days of Jesus and Socrates, it is still not quite safe because rulers and insecure people are fearful of free people.

"You need not advertise what you are doing. You could quietly practice in your daily life by taking small, unobtrusive steps, like a child learning to stand up and walk. Keep your promises and refrain from making promises that you may not be able to keep. Courageously face the consequences, however painful they might be. Do not mislead anyone. When you diligently *practice* this path, you will naturally learn to maintain your feelings, thoughts, words, and actions in harmony.

"Be true to your innate nature, which is your best teacher and guide. Take responsibility for your emotions. When your feelings, thoughts, words, and actions are aligned, then they will be naturally balanced. It would be right for you even if you get rebuked or punished by society. You will be at peace even if the entire world is against you. *You are your best and only role model that nature has created.* It will be the beginning of a learning process that will eventually lead to the exposure of illusions and revelation of the truth that liberates.

"It is likely that you will encounter great difficulties in the initial stages of practicing the first four steps. If you are diligent, you will quickly recognize any mistakes you may have committed and learn never to repeat them. You will naturally become strong to face the real world without intentionally hurting anyone. It is an iterative process that requires patience, commitment, and persistence."

5. Balanced or non-exploitative living (*Samma-Ajiva*)

The Buddha resumed his discourse on the path of truth. "The next two stages are related to your livelihood. Balanced or non-exploitative living (*Samma-Ajiva*) requires that you live without harming others. You fulfill the first principle.

6. Balanced Vocation (*Samma-Vayama*)

"Balanced Vocation or Occupation refers to taking up a profession that does not exploit or harm others. Find an occupation where you can satisfy your existential and creative needs without violating the first principle.

"The first six milestones are valuable for the educational system. It would be relatively easy to inculcate these practices at school because they would come naturally to the young. Children will gravitate toward what is natural to them if there are no obstacles. It would be hard to correct those mistakes later in life.

7. Balanced Mindfulness (*Samma-Sati*)

"Balanced Mindfulness (*Samma-Sati*) is the penultimate milestone. You now turn inwards with mindfulness, introspection, and meditation. It is time to check whether you have covered all the milestones. Each milestone has to be reviewed carefully to make sure that your feelings, thoughts, words, and actions are aligned with your emotions as well as your external human inter-actions. Become mindful through meditation.

8. Complete Balance (*Samma-Samadhi*)

"The last milestone is the destination. You will naturally realize it when you arrive. Complete or Total Balance (Samma-Samadhi) is a completely relaxed and serene mind without any kind of judgment or acquisitive desire, positive or negative. It is a state of nothingness or nirvana. It is exactly what Patanjali described as samadhi.

"These eight milestones, when covered, will reveal that there is no suffer-ing other than that which is brought about by oneself. There is nothing more to be done at this stage. Mindfulness will eventually awaken you to the true nature of reality, as your mind is naturally aligned with your innate nature and dhamma, and life flows smoothly.

"My teachings follow the modern scientific principles used in active control of dynamic systems with negative feedback (Franklin 1994). The objective is to reduce errors (energy dissipation) to zero. In the case of the mind, the goal is to reduce mental disturbances at every stage. At the seventh milestone, people may experience an impasse, as if left in the doldrums. It is impossible to cross the barrier through logical intellectualization. It is possible to intuitively realize nirvana when compassion and empathy arise in your heart. The transition to nirvana occurs intuitively, just like a child learns to ride a bicycle.

"Let me now move to the third part of my approach: practical **experimentation**."

The Practice

"To guide people along, I asked them to become mendicants. It naturally creates qualities of compassion and empathy, when you observe how kind and supportive others are in giving you alms without expecting anything in return.

"You do not have to become a beggar in the conventional sense. You become a thankful receiver of help, which you do get anyway in any walk of life. For example, you get paid for what you do, which is helpful in fulfill-ing your need for food, shelter, etc. Receive it with gratitude. Receive every-thing that nature offers with innate thankfulness. Whether we admit it or not, whether we realize it or not, and whether we portray ourselves as beggars or not, we receive help from nature, and it is given unconditionally. Be thankful for every gift, big or small, you receive from anyone. The realization of this unconditional love from nature and being thankful is what Muhammad referred to as *shukriya*. This very mental state will land you at the eighth milestone of nirvana.

"It is not your brain and intellect, but your heart that will land you there. You could go to the end of the world searching for nirvana with your intellect and not find it. Whereas, you do not even have to take a single step to find it in your heart. It is just a matter of attitude. There is nothing to think or do. Just being in this state is enough. It is not logic or reason, but emotion and empathy that will help you bridge the gap and reach the destination of nirvana or truth that liberates."

Jesus in Jerusalem

Bridging the Gap

Jesus's teachings are easy to understand. It is hard to misinterpret simple messages such as "show your other cheek," "love your enemy," "love your neighbor," "be forgiving," etc. and mistake them for revenge, massacre, enslavement, lynching, burning on stakes, etc. The difficulty is not in their interpretation, but in their implementation.

Even a child knows that following his teachings could make us a doormat. If we show the other cheek, we will be easy target for bullies. If we are meek, enemies will run roughshod over us. We may not even be alive to forgive them. We cannot be generous if we are poor. Hardly anyone wants to be a saint or a martyr; these titles seem to be a way that society seems to manipulate and exploit people by boosting their egos or self-images. The tragic fate that overtook his life itself is a huge impediment to have faith in his teachings.

The gap between his teachings and practice cannot be bridged by reciting chapter and verse from the Book. It is necessary to know what exactly a compassionate figure like Jesus intended to accomplish by sending his followers in the perceived harm's way. A whole new world will open up for those who have an indefatigable urge to realize the true meaning and purpose of his teachings through diligent practice and **experimentation**.

The Life and Message of Jesus

The Sermon on the Mount contains some of the most sublime and radical insights ever conveyed. His life and teachings are infinitely more meaningful and valuable when his life is viewed as that of an ordinary human being with extraordinary insights than putting him on a pedestal and ignoring his message. Treating him as a friend allows us to understand the meaning and purpose of his teachings through our own **experimentation**.

His approach is fearless. His teachings would guide one to liberation at the speed of light if the seeker has the courage and commitment. A logical explanation may not be there, but his teachings touch the deepest chord and resonate within us because his insights reflect our innate nature. I approached Jesus and requested that he share the salient features of his life and teachings with me, as I wanted to know him directly as an ordinary human being without associating miracles and mythical beings with him.

I was interested in knowing if there was any extraordinary incident in his life that led to the revelation. "According to religious texts, Abraham and Moses were visited by God himself. Devas from heaven sprinkled flowers on the Buddha to celebrate his realization of nirvana, and the angel Gabriel revealed the Koran to Muhammad. Who inspired you?"

"I did not have such exalted experiences," Jesus responded quietly. "There was no high point and, if anything, it was, perhaps, the lowest point that had the greatest impact on my life. I had a gut-wrenching experience in the marketplace that mirrored my own hidden flaws and opened my eyes to the truth that liberated me. Until then, I was blind to my own shortcomings but was keenly aware of the faults in others. The experience that I am about to narrate has never been revealed before. It took me to the depths of darkness. It might resonate within you and liberate you and others who hear it."

"Here's my story, which brought me down from my high horse but miraculously saved me," said Jesus with deep emotion. "I was born in a society where adultery was punishable by stoning to death. I grew up in a society that severely looked down on children born out of wedlock. As I was one, my childhood and adolescence were a difficult period as I was taunted by my peers and denied normal friendship. I missed out on all the fun that young adults experience. A deep resentment for my mother took roots within me, as I saw her as the primary cause of my miserable life.

"Finding no joy in such a society, I became an introvert. I traveled far and wide to learn more about life. I saw similar problems everywhere. Women were subjugated and female infanticide was common. People were servile toward the Roman rulers and led a fearful, anxious, and insecure life that was prone to deception and hostility. I turned to religion to find solace but saw a big gap between precepts and practices of priests, who misinterpreted scriptures. I decided to become a rabbi and bring back the glory of the Torah.

"I noticed that Judaism had become corrupt. I was upset by what was practiced in the temple, where business interests took precedence. As you might have read, I overturned the tables of moneychangers and hawkers in the temple. I was dismayed by the arrogance of the high priests who were colluding with the Roman rulers. Just as I was beginning to feel self-righteous and preparing to teach them a lesson, a gut-wrenching event occurred that completely changed my life. It taught me the true meaning of the Torah.

"I observed a frenzied crowd around a woman who was about to be stoned to death for adultery. By a mysterious coincidence or because they knew that I aspired to be a rabbi, I was asked to pronounce my judgment according to the religious scriptures. They probably expected me to approve stoning her to death as per the prevailing practices of Judaism, but I knew that stoning to death was cruel and the Ten Commandments prohibited killing. The Torah taught that we must not do to others that which is hateful if done to us. Besides, she had only submitted herself to desires that did nobody any harm. The simple woman was trembling with fear, facing a painful death."

"I still shudder when I recall that scene," said Jesus. "It hit me like a million thunderbolts. I did not see an adulterous woman about to be stoned to death but saw my mother in her. I saw in her my mother who had probably experienced similar passion in her youth but who had taken such good care of me with the support of my father. She was such a wonderful human being against whom I held a deep grudge based on my selfish and self-righteous perspectives. I had carried a deep resentment against her all my life. I felt crestfallen and terribly ashamed of myself. I realized how ungrateful and unjust I was to my loving mother all my life. I had failed to uphold the fifth commandment. I did not practice the very precepts that I was planning to preach as a rabbi.

"I realized that love was the source of all life. Moral codes of societies, codes that were imposed by avaricious rulers and loveless priests, are driven by the desire to control and exploit others for material wealth, power, and social capital. *Morals are worthless in the absence of love, kindness, and compassion, and irrelevant in their presence.*"

Jesus continued, "I recognized that in my heart I had deeply hurt my parents and especially my mother, and nobody else except I knew about it. It was the saddest and also the most cathartic moment in my life when I was flooded with love for my mother. I realized her unconditional love for me. I deeply repented. My resentment vanished instantly only to be replaced with a deep love for my mother in particular, and all women in general. They are my real *gurus*. Judgment and condemnation were replaced by love, empathy, and compassion. A huge burden was lifted off my shoulders and set me free. At that moment I knew that repentance, love, empathy, and compassion would set everyone free.

"I realized that I could not lift a pebble to kill this woman even if my life was at stake," said Jesus. "It would have been like killing my mother to whom I owed my life. I saw in this woman a mother like my own. I could not kill her. I realized that everyone was born to a mother who engaged in sex. The only difference was that one was granted legality by the clergy, the rulers, and society while the other was free but illegal. One had a certificate from society and the other didn't. What a sham! Do you need approval from society to love another being? Sex is a natural component of love, the source of life. Tears welled up in my eyes. I asked the one who was not born to a mother to cast the first stone.

"The crowd dispersed, as everyone was born to a mother."

It was a touching incident, which made Jesus very human. It underscored the need to recognize one's own flaws and repent, which thoroughly cleanses the mind. It was indeed a powerful moment in his life. He hit the bottom only to bounce back to the very peak of consciousness. Tears welled up in my eyes too to hear his deeply moving experience.

After a brief pause to recover his feelings, and let me recover mine, Jesus continued. "I discovered the destructive nature of judgment and condemnation based on man-made moral values, which were usually imposed on people by rulers and priests. Morals are all about logic and reason but have little to do with love and compassion, which are innate to human beings. There is no need to impose morals on loving and compassionate people because their actions are naturally good and moral. It is more important to guide people to discover and express the power of love and creativity that is hidden within. I also realized the power of repentance to cleanse the mind of past mistakes.

"Repentance and compassion became the main theme of my sermons. I realized that compassion was the cement that held the structure (body and mind) together.

"*The practice of the Ten Commandments accompanied by compassion is the truth that liberates.*

"Violation of a commandment was not to be treated with condemnation and punishment, but with understanding and guidance. It is the lack of compassion and its replacement by judgment based on logic and reason with revenge and punishment that makes people lead a hypocritical life in fear and anxiety."

"You must resist the temptation to convert hypocritical politicians and priests into honest and caring human beings," continued Jesus. "Be kind, but don't patronize or condemn. They live in a different world where ignorance is mistaken for knowledge, and cleverness for intelligence.

"Leaders will eventually follow the right path when they have no followers. They think that they are leaders because they see others running after them begging for favors. Stop chasing them. Have faith in nature and leave that responsibility to her. She knows what she is doing. Instead, begin with your own individual liberation.

"If you are driven by fear, find its root cause within yourself. Fear will never disappear as long as you believe its source to be outside of you. It is like the ghost in the lamppost. Fear will vanish in the presence of truth like the mist in the presence of the rising sun. Be courageous. Have faith in your innate nature."

"As you are aware," Jesus continued, "The Buddha was able to elaborate on his teachings for over four decades, which enabled him to negate dualistic interpretation of his teachings. As he himself observed, he had an intelligent counterpart in Vimalakirti who was able to offer contrarian views to demolish dualistic dogmas held by his disciples. In spite of it, Buddhism split into many denominations.

"As my life was cut short, I did not have the opportunity to expound on my insights. Ignorant theologians introduced dualistic concepts of good and evil, heaven and hell, sin and virtue, angel and devil, saint and sinner, reward and punishment, etc. Fictitious ideas of the virgin birth, Son of God, resurrection, and miracles were used to further reinforce ignorance. Rules against blasphemy, heresy, and apostasy were used to suppress attempts to elucidate the truth that went against the perceived interests of clergy and rulers. Christianity split into a gazillion mutually exclusive denominations.

"However, the past is past. You know by now how disastrous it could be when dualistic logic is used to justify evil actions in the name of (the son of) God. It is time to repent for past mistakes and resume with a clean slate. The teachings are as relevant today when understood in a non-dualistic manner without invoking mythical gods or doctrines."

The Sermon on the Mount

"I shall now describe the essence of the teachings," continued Jesus. "The focus was to expose internal contradictions (ignorance) and guide people to liberation.

"In conventional dualistic thinking you are taught how to climb the social ladder at any cost. It has a tendency to dissipate energy that manifests as fear, anxiety, insecurity, guilt, and mental suffering. Instead, I encouraged my followers to shun the ambitions of climbing up the dissipative and subservient social ladder and instead start climbing down to find their innate nature at the center and be free. Going down takes little or no effort, but the fear of a precipitous fall creates a tendency to cling.

"When you pursue this path, you may be perceived as being meek, weak, poor, and vulnerable by the rest of society, which is intent on going up the ladder in search of wealth and power using lies, deception, greed, and covetousness, which are mistaken for strength. *Social climbers would feel exposed and push you further down and thereby help you go down faster toward truth and liberation. So, love your enemies!*

"I was certainly aware of the travails that diligent seekers are likely to go through while practicing my teachings. Teachings are not meant to be a condition for being recognized as a saint or martyr. These are the milestones along the amazing journey to liberation. This is not idle speculation but a certainty. When you practice the teachings, you are exposed to the dangers that compel you to become strong.

"A ferocious lion may kill a beautiful deer, but you do not judge the lion to be evil. A lion acts naturally but a human being acts cruelly because of ignorance, which is a mental affliction. Become strong enough that even cruel people do not mess with you. A few of them may even turn around and seek your guidance to be liberated. Diligent practice will compel you to become strong to fearlessly face the world. Only the strong and liberated can be truly forgiving, compassionate, and kind toward others.

"My approach helps those with *feeling* as the dominant cognitive function. These are the people who are generous, kind, caring, and compassionate. However, in an exploitative society, they face huge problems in expressing themselves without getting hurt in the process. My teachings, when implemented, will compel such people to bolster their *thinking* and *sensing* functions to express themselves freely and without the fear of being hurt in the process. The truth will be naturally revealed when *feeling, sensing* and *thinking* are equally strong and balanced, and your *feelings, thoughts, words, and actions are in harmony.*

"Let us briefly look at the Sermon," (in italics), continued Jesus.

1. Fulfilling the Law

Do not think that I came to destroy the Law. I did not come to destroy but to fulfill.

"I was not referring to the laws imposed by the rulers. I was referring to the eternal principle (davar) that governs our emotions. You cannot violate any law of nature. You have no choice but to fulfill it. You can become aware of the nature of the law only through practice and **experimentation**.

"You must make bold experiments with your emotions. Awareness of the law and living in accordance with it is the truth that liberates."

2. Go the Second Mile

I tell you not to resist evil. Whoever slaps you on your cheek offer the other also. If anyone wants to take away your tunic, let him have your cloak also. And whoever forces you to go one mile, volunteer to go with him two. Give to him who asks.

"The aim is not to become a saint or martyr but to learn from experience. This teaching is to create a dire situation for yourself and learn how to deal with it without getting hurt and without hurting others.

"I did not want you to get slapped by everyone. It was to make you understand from direct experience that such actions usually have consequences that will hurt you. You must realize the weaknesses within you that allow others dare to hurt you. Others are your sparring partners, where you get hit as a part of the training. You could keep the damage within tolerable limits by starting the **experimentation** in a small way.

"Whatever the negative response from others, I want you to work on eliminating your weakness instead of judging them. You must become internally strong and unshakable.

"Initially, it may be difficult to go that extra mile or give that cloak without getting hurt, but to be a martyr must not be an option. The right solution is to develop the ability to help others without getting hurt in the process. If you are strong, you could go that extra mile without getting hurt and also help the other to become strong. To become strong, you have to be aware of the environment. To know the environment, you must be able to think and function in a rational manner. You will be able to implement my teachings only if you strengthen your *thinking* and *sensing* functions by becoming a productive, independent, and strong individual. Coupled with your innately strong *feeling* function, they will create inner balance and harmony to reveal the truth that liberates."

3. Love Your Enemies

Love your enemies, bless those who curse you, be kind to those who hate you, and be merciful to those who persecute you.

"Nature has no enemies. As a part of nature, you too have no enemies. Those who try to harm you are ignorant of their own innate nature. However, they are helping you along the way to truth and liberation. Your perceived enemies accurately expose your weaknesses, as they are always focused on them. They give you free professional consultations! It is then up to you to strengthen your weaker functions and create mental balance.

"Torei Zenji, a disciple of Hakuin, one of the greatest Zen masters, made a similar statement when he said that you must treat your enemies as if they were Buddhas in the clothing of enemies trying to help you.

"These teachings must not be treated as if I am trying to condone evil doers or forgiving them in a saintly manner. Loving your enemies is an utterly selfish action because it lets you become keenly aware of your weaknesses so that you can take pragmatic steps to strengthen those areas. Enemies act as a pure mirror. What you hate in them is an exact reflection of the source of your weakness. If you eliminate that weakness, you will be free and immune to external threats, and thus have no enemies.

"You must be composed enough to see that those who are trying to commit evil deeds are themselves suffering from fear and insecurity and are emotionally unfulfilled. At the same time, they are unintentionally forcing you to become strong. You will be able to help others overcome fear and insecurity only when you are strong, free, and fearless. They expose you to yourself.

"Don't treat this teaching as a moral value to be brandished in social gatherings. You must practice until you are truly liberated and look with gratitude at others, friends, and enemies alike, as teachers who have come to guide you in their own ways."

4. Doing Good is an End in Itself

Do not trumpet your generosity. When you do a charitable deed, do not let your left hand know what your right hand is doing.

"The only good you can do to others is to wake them up from their nightmares," observed Jesus. "They are likely to be upset when you try to awaken them but that is the price you pay for waking them up from a burning home. It is your innate nature. Nature thrives on sharing and compassion. It is how nature is set up. It is a joyful experience when you are true to yourself. The purpose is served in the act itself.

"The realization of compassion is the first and last step to liberation. When you diligently follow your innate nature, your inborn intelligence will guide you to strengthen your *thinking* and *sensing* functions because you will get hurt if you practice compassion without being strong. Improve your skills to fulfill your innate nature without getting hurt in the process."

5. Do Not Worry

Nature will meet your needs. Do not worry about tomorrow.

"Nature cares for you and nourishes life. Therefore, do not worry and say, what shall we eat? or what shall we drink? or what shall we wear? Nature knows that you need all these things. Leave that responsibility to her and lead an anxiety-free life. Be joyful and lead a free and fearless life today. *Que sera, sera*! Whatever will be, will be!

"Nature has given you the gift of mercy and compassion with the hope that you will implement it. She has given you the intelligence to effectively take care of your biological, physiological, and psychological needs. Make creative use of your *thinking* and *sensing* functions and enjoy the process that will lead to mental balance and liberation."

6. Do Not Judge

Judge not, lest ye be judged. Do not complain about the speck of dust in your brother's eye, when you have a log in your own eye.

"It is one of the oft-quoted, most misunderstood, and invariably violated teachings. It is not an indictment on judgment. One can judge as much as one pleases, but it is baseless without a uniformly valid frame of reference for the dualistic values on which it is assumed to rest. Usually, judgment is merely an attempt to establish your superiority, which arises from an inferiority complex. Doctors do not condemn patients; they diagnose and cure their ailments. Judgment, as in condemnation, is a clear indication of a lack of love or concern.

"There are three types of judgments. The first is the one exhibited by parents, teachers, and well-wishers. A mother uses it to prevent the child from harming herself/himself and teachers grade students to help them understand their strengths and weaknesses in a subject. This judgement is based on love and concern. The second kind of judgement is just being factual. To call a spade a spade is also a judgment, but it is neutral. It provides information for people to either use or ignore. Encouraging a person with well-earned praise also belongs to this category. The third type of judgment is condemnation or flattery with an intent to cause harm or gain benefits at someone's expense. The first two types of judgment do not violate *the first principle*, but the third one does.

"It is more important to understand the source of judgment within you. You may find that your criticism and condemnation often arise from fear and insecurity and a perceived need to control others, but rarely from a concern for the other. A mother may judge her child and even express anger out of love in an effort to enforce discipline and make her/him strong to deal with social pressures, but when a son or daughter judges with anger, it may not be out of concern for the mother but because of perceived opposition to selfish desires.

"Outwardly, both judgment and anger may appear similar, but the important point is to know your emotions. Is it a selfish effort to manipulate and control or is it out of genuine concern for the other? The two actions are polar opposites although both can be classified as judgments. I could be logically accused of judgment because I was doing it all the time, but my objective was to liberate people, and not because I wanted to be treated like a Messiah.

"There is no need to be afraid of being judged. It is always good to know your flaws so that you can eliminate them. If you judge, do so as it might help the other to recognize and overcome an existing flaw. Before you help others, make sure that you are strong in the first place. It will be more effective if you make sure that the other is also receptive. There is no point in forcing it on unwilling people. Leave the final decision to nature; she knows best.

"Judgment arises when you cling to self-image. It disappears with the realization that we are all part of the same reality and there is no *other* to judge. Judgment is a clear indication of the presence of self-image. When the self-image disappears, feelings, thoughts, words, and actions will naturally be in harmony."

7. Keep Asking, Seeking, Knocking

Ask, and it will be given to you; seek, and you will find; knock, and it will be opened to you.

"What is 'It', you might wonder," continued Jesus. "Rabindranath Tagore made a beautiful distinction (Tagore 1919), 'those who *want to love*, knock on the door and those who are *in love*, find the door open.' Of course, I couldn't agree more.

"The door is not out there as one might imagine, and it is not a door that needs to be opened by someone else. It is your heart that remains closed, which needs to be opened. Love is the key. It remains shut when your heart is starved of love. Your mind feels suffocated inside a prison and wants to gain freedom. It is not a door through which you enter. It is a door through which you leave and find the freedom to express your playfulness and explore the universe in a creative manner. When you are in love, you'll find the door open. Loving yourself is not to be seen with the negative connotation of narcissism. It is a tribute to nature. Life is such a miracle and how she has created it is simply mind-boggling and wonderful. It is an expression of love and gratitude to nature for giving us this opportunity to experience it.

"A judgmental mind tends to compartmentalize the world into exclusive clubs based on tribe, religion, wealth, education, nation, gender, race, etc. It is the source of prejudice, hypocrisy, and bigotry. Empty your mental storage boxes that are filled with garbage. Besides being an unnecessary burden that you carry wherever you go, the contents rot and cause you suffering. Fear, anxiety, insecurity, and suffering will vanish instantly when these boxes are obliterated. Recognize that when your heart is shut, even the most generous and benevolent nature has no way of entering it to transmit her endless energy. An open, compassionate heart is the door through which nature pours her energy into you.

"Love naturally eliminates fear of the outside world when you realize that it is also a part of you. You are not afraid of what you love. You are only afraid of what you dislike or hate. When you venture out with feelings of love, you will find the universe welcoming you. Of course, when you cling to your self-image that is apart from the rest of nature, you will also perceive others trying to destroy you. Thus, you must first focus on becoming strong to venture out, not because you are afraid but because you have the desire to express your love for beings. If you are weak and venture into a jungle, you might be eaten by lions. However, if you are strong, you could even protect them from harm. Again, this teaching will also compel you to maintain balance among all your cognitive functions."

8. The Narrow Way

Enter by the narrow gate; for wide is the gate and broad is the road that leads to destruction, and there are many who go in by it. Because narrow is the gate and difficult is the road which leads to life, and there are few who find it.

"People who seek safety in numbers have created hell on earth. The path to liberation is narrow. A camel may pass through an eye of a needle, but it is impossible to enter heaven with an intellect that is rich with information and knowledge based on logic and reason. It is a problem faced by both religious followers and atheistic philosophers. The narrow way requires the innocence and trusting nature of a child with no self-image.

"*The path to heaven is through the heart and not the intellect.*

"The path is so narrow that it has no dimensions. Hence, only an individual with zero dimensions or no-self (anatta), as correctly expressed by the Buddha, can pass through it. The objective is not to destroy yourself but realize that your self-image is a fiction that is given a semblance of reality by your conditioned mind. It is best to get rid of the illusion but, unfortunately, you cannot get rid of it with logic, reason, or knowledge, the very tools that have actually created the illusion. The only way to overcome this paradoxical problem is through intuition.

"Normally, you use your self-image to increase your social, political, and economic capital. You will need none of them when you are self-sufficient and balanced. When you meditate on this problem you will intuitively find the right approach. When you lose everything (false images of the self and others), you will gain everything (the true nature of reality). Nature will supply all the energy you need when you are centered. No energy is wasted through mental stress. You will naturally and effortlessly fulfill all your emotional needs. A return to childlike innocence is the most effective path to the realization of this truth that liberates."

9. You Will Know Them by Their Fruits

Beware of false prophets, who are wolves that come to you in sheep's clothing. You will know them by their actions.

"I did not say this. I was not interested in spreading fear but guiding you to fearlessness and liberation. This message was conveyed by well-intentioned people out of concern for you to be aware of charlatans masquerading as teachers. There is no need to worry about prophets, true or false. If you are true to yourself, you cannot be deceived.

"Forget about false prophets; you don't need any prophet. You don't need me or my teachings. You don't need the Buddha or his teachings. You don't need Muhammad or his teachings. If we could find a way, so can you. Nature has equipped you with innate intelligence to meet any challenge. Apply yourself diligently to the task. Use our teachings as a friendly guide for diligent **exploration** of the mind and practical **experimentation**.

"Socrates said that an unexamined life is not worth living.

"A life of fear and fetter is not worth living. Remember that all this effort is only to find ways to express yourself creatively as you explore the universe. You want a playful environment where everyone is sharing their creative potential with you in this wonderful journey called life. Align yourself with your innate nature. Be balanced and enjoy a fearless and fulfilling ride."

10. Build on The Rock

Whoever hears my teachings and practices them is like a man who builds his house on the rock. It remains intact even in the presence of hurricanes and floods. Anyone who hears my teachings and does not practice them is like a man who builds his house on sand. It would collapse like a house of cards in the presence of wind and flood.

"This last observation is vital. If you merely memorize the teachings and preach without practicing, you will suffer as a hypocrite. You will judge and condemn others merely because they are not as well informed. You will condemn the followers of other religions just as they would condemn you. The result would be a disaster for both. The mere recitation of the teachings without practice leads to cruel deeds: crusades, inquisitions, colonization, slavery, apartheid, impaling, burning of women, the subordination of women, genocide, jihad, violent wars, and terrorism.

"My teachings are not meant to create wars but to bring peace. It has not happened because of people who have not practiced the teachings.

"It is still not too late. If nature intends to wipe you out, she could do so in an instant by sending an asteroid or a pandemic your way. Your problems are self-created. The purpose of the teachings is not Armageddon, but to guide people to a peaceful life where every individual can explore and express creativity in a playful manner.

"It must be obvious to you that when every individual is liberated through the practice of the teachings, there will be no need for showing your other cheek or forgiving someone. Poverty and meekness will have no meaning. There will be no need for virtue or morality. There will be no enemies. Playfulness and joyful creativity will be the only chores in your life when you are free. The teachings will guide you from here to the other shore, but you cannot get there without diligent practice and without helping others along the way. It is the simplest and yet the most effective path to liberation. It does not require religious scholarship or academic brilliance. Even a child could understand it. In fact, only a childlike individual understands this path.

Active Control with Positive Feedback

"My approach entails significant risk. Active control with positive feedback takes a system rapidly to one of two possible extremes, depending on how it is implemented. It is also prone to instability. Thus, it is a risky approach if one lacks clarity. One could end in heaven or eternal hell. Positive feedback rapidly leads to a zero-one situation. You either become liberated or turn into a charlatan, depending on whether you implement or exploit the teachings to fulfill selfish desires by exploiting others.

"Positive feedback amplifies, intensifies, and enhances the process to rapidly reach the desired result (Franklin 1994). For example, according to medical researchers, the Ferguson Reflex that describes the process of childbirth is a biological application of positive feedback. When a contraction occurs, the hormone oxytocin causes a nerve stimulus, which stimulates the hypothalamus to produce more oxytocin, which increases uterine contractions, increasing in amplitude and frequency until childbirth is complete. Positive feedback could also quickly lead to the exact opposite of the desired results. Many deleterious habits such as alcoholism, addiction to drugs, smoking, pornography, junk food, gambling, etc. are also based on positive feedback with dopamine playing a critical role.

"As in the case of engineering systems, this approach is also the riskiest because an improper application would take the follower in the exact opposite direction. It is clear that the destruction will be great if you do not practice the teachings.

"At the other extreme, when diligently implemented, this approach has led to unprecedented levels of magnanimity, charity, generosity, and compassion among those who have faithfully followed the teachings. The remarkable generosity shown by the people in the West, especially the USA, can be attributed to the practices that have been ingrained in them by compassionate parents and priests. The millennials are now moving toward deeper realms by being compassionate toward animals and the environment. It seems to be a natural process of human evolution to a higher potential.

"Many great poets, composers, and artists in the world have practiced my teachings. The path of devotion is primarily meant for people with *feeling* as their dominant cognitive function. It is a path of compassion, empathy, and harmony, which are the emotions that are behind love and caring. Love and caring need not be restricted to life. They may extend to the arts, literature, science, and anything in which you could get lost.

"Practice the following steps and realize liberation that occurs in a paradoxical manner.

"Firstly, you must practice the first principle, '*Do not do to others what you would not want others to do to you.*'

"Secondly, you must have utmost faith in nature, realizing that she is the one that created you and her nature is to nurture you. Do not be concerned about tomorrow. It does not mean that you must simply sit idle and someone will feed you. Your innate nature will guide you to do what needs to be done without anxiety and without harming others.

"Thirdly, and most importantly, you must treat the teachings as methods to get rid of your false perceptions of reality (illusions or ignorance). You still need to work for and take care of your basic biological needs. The adverse social order poses challenges that will compel you to be mentally and physically strong to deal with adversity as well as to deter others from messing with you, but that is how you must interpret my approach."

Muhammad in Mecca

The Life and Message of Muhammad

Muhammad's succinct message of peace, mercy, compassion, and camaraderie can transform the world into heaven if everyone practices them.

According to Islamic texts (Armstrong 1992), Muhammad was brought up by his uncle in Mecca. His personal integrity and keen business acumen attracted the attention of his employer Khadijah, a rich, older, and wise widow who married him. His uncle and wife belonged to the elite of Mecca. His early life had little to suggest the unfolding of subsequent events, which changed the course of human history in a dramatic manner.

Muhammad had the habit of meditating for hours in the cave Hira, contemplating on the social order in Mecca where religion was big business, there was slavery, women were subjugated, female infanticide was common, and the autocratic rulers were constantly engaged in violent conflicts with other tribes. Like the Buddha, he was also probably seeking an answer to end the widespread malaise.

Suddenly one day, the true nature of the problem and its solution were revealed to him. He anticipated serious repercussions because he did not expect the news to be well-received by the rulers. He came home and confided in his loving wife. The courageous and wise Khadijah comforted him and encouraged him to share his precious insights with others regardless of the consequences. He did, and the rest is history.

I requested of Muhammad that he describe what happened in the cave. "What did you discover that made you so excited? It has had a huge impact on human history, not all of it, perhaps, as you might have intended. I am eager. Please, enlighten."

Happy as always, Muhammad responded, "I was ecstatic when I realized the need for universal camaraderie, the emancipation of women, and the abolition of slavery. I was immensely overjoyed at the prospect. Women are the primary caregivers in any society. I realized that all wars and conflicts are due to mutual animosity and distrust. Universal camaraderie would inevitably bring universal peace along with it. I realized that Allah was most merciful and compassionate in taking care of all human needs. It only required human cooperation to feed and shelter all of humanity.

"The idea of universal brotherhood and emancipation of women was revolutionary in an era when their subjugation, slavery, and tribal conflicts were common. Even in the US, where freedom is highly valued and etched in its constitution, slavery was not abolished until the middle of the nineteenth century, a full twelve centuries after me. It took another half-a-century for women to get the right to vote. Universal suffrage took another fifty years before African American men and women were able to freely exercise their voting rights.

"Racism is still rampant in the United States. Fascism led to the Second World War. Women are repressed in many parts of the world. Sectarian conflicts are widespread. Today, almost fourteen centuries later, universal camaraderie is still a distant dream.

"I was dismayed by the presence of slavery, which was quite entrenched in Mecca, where I lived. It provided social as well as economic capital for the wealthy and powerful rulers. I knew that they would be against the idea of universal camaraderie, just as the big banks would be opposed to interest-free loans and weapons manufacturers would be opposed to world peace.

"Secondly, I realized that there was an invariant, inviolable omnipotent, omniscient, and omnipresent law or eternal principle that governed creation

144

and all life. Abraham called the law *davar* and the origin of creation as Yhwh, but Judaism converted Yhwh into a supernatural god. Christians converted it into a fictitious trinity.

"I did not want to revert to a mythical God. So, I first denied God and introduced Allah. I emphasized that there was no God and there was only Allah. In spite of this precaution, the clergy converted even Allah into a supernatural deity. Allah went the same way as Yhwh, as people started believing that Allah is the only real God and all others are fake.

"Thirdly, as Allah is impartial, there was no need for image worship. Hence, I rejected image worship and asked my disciples to focus on understanding the nature of the law and live in accordance with it. Sadly, people idolize and worship the images and symbols of the rulers. Every government office is filled with photographs of the rulers, every street is filled with their statues, and every building is topped by a tribal flag. I was opposed to the worship of all images, forms, and symbols.

"It brings me to the fourth principle, which describes the nature of Allah. I found Allah to be most merciful and compassionate. Imagine living in a hot and arid desert. Allah created an oasis where you could find a verdant pasture, palms and dates to provide healthy food, shade to protect you from the hot sun, and water to quench your thirst. Allah created all the wonderful plants, vegetables, and fruits to feed your hunger. How wonderfully merciful and compassionate is Allah. I fell in love when I realized the most caring and generous qualities of Allah.

"What happens to you when you come across such love? You surrender. You submit to Allah, knowing full well that Allah cares for you, protects you, feeds you, and provides everything that you need, just like a mother. I called the experience Islam, as worries vanished and were replaced by immense peace. I saw that anyone who realized the true qualities of Allah will be naturally peaceful, compassionate, and creative."

"What happened next?" I asked.

"As expected, the priests and rulers of Mecca did not like what I conveyed. They were afraid of losing the wealth and power provided by slavery, image worship, and religious rituals. Universal camaraderie would wipe out their special status. Filled with fear, anxiety, and insecurity they tried to nip the movement in the bud. My influential uncle and wise wife protected me as long as they were alive. When they died in quick succession, the rulers felt free to assassinate me. I escaped to Yathrib (Medina). They came after me there too, but I was amazed to see what free people with courage and commitment could accomplish even with little monetary and military resources. Eventually, when I returned to Mecca, it was done without shedding any blood. It brought peace to Mecca during my life. An ordinary, poor boy of Mecca unexpectedly became its ruler because his message of peace, mercy, compassion, and camaraderie resonated among the people.

"Allah is for peace and harmony among all people. Allah is for universal camaraderie, mercy, compassion, and charity. Allah does not discriminate. Jihad is an inner struggle to realize peace and not a violent conflict with other religions."

"We are watching in frustration how events unfold," I said. "What would you advise?"

"I am glad you asked," continued Muhammad. "Many people, including Muslims, have misunderstood my actions. I was living in a world where might was seen as right. Peace had no chance except if it favored the ruler, who stood above the law. Ordinary, peaceful people were subdued by fear and violence, and did not have the resources to set things right.

"For over ten years, I tried to spread the understanding of Allah. When rulers tried to destroy me and my peaceful followers, I pursued the four-step approach, viz., *'saama dhaana bheda dandam,'* which Krishna described earlier. I began with peaceful negotiation (*saama*); then made generous offers (*dhaana*); when that too failed, I tried to explain the nature of the conflict (*bheda*), and when all these failed, I used the stick (*dandam*) as a last resort when they tried to destroy my peaceful followers.

"I could have shown the other cheek like Jesus. His disciples were sensitive feelers. His approach was to make them both physically and mentally strong, but he was killed before he could complete his mission. In stark contrast, my followers were action-oriented people with *sensing* as their dominant cognitive function, who needed to strengthen their *feeling* and *thinking* functions.

"I did not shy away from a good fight if it was aligned with my innate nature. Like Krishna, I used the only language rogues understood, with immense sadness, and not as a way to fulfill greed or to seek revenge. When I became powerful, I was able to convert Mecca into Islam, a land of peace, without shedding any blood. My objectives were no different from those of the Buddha and Jesus.

"You sought my advice for the present world. Physical strength does not play a major role in human interactions today. You have several democracies where ordinary people have the power to effect a change. You have fewer dictatorships. Slavery has been practically abolished. Even racism has been recognized as evil and is being eliminated. Significant social progress has taken place during the intervening years.

"My two teachings are simple, straightforward, and every individual can implement them without external authority:

Don't do to others what would be hateful if it were done to you.

Keep your feelings, thoughts, words, actions, and emotions aligned with each other.

"My approach, like that of Abraham, expects you to strictly adhere to the first principle: '*Do not do to others what you would not want them to do to you.*' It will force you to *think* before you act. It will also create empathy and kindness within you when you observe how blind acts of cruelty cause pain and suffering to innocent people.

"You cannot help humanity by being deceptive and cruel. Stop dropping bombs from drones that kill innocent civilians, while you and your loved ones sit safely in a bunker. If you believe in a fight, lead from the front. Be honest and be brave. Otherwise, you are no different from the ones that you are fighting against.

"Secondly, explore, experiment, and *maintain feelings, thoughts, words, and actions in harmony.* It eliminates mental disturbances and makes you fearless. It brings you peace, which you can then spread among all of humanity. Work toward universal camaraderie with mercy and compassion. *Build bridges and not walls.*

"You have made some progress, but you still have a long way to go.

"Worldwide movements like Black Lives Matter (BLM) indicate that the conscience of a large segment of population is finally awakened. It was thrilling to watch a cricket test series between England and the West Indies in July 2020 begin with a "Knee" in support of BLM. People are waking up from the nightmare that hurts everyone.

"The best place to start is at home. The US is the most prosperous country in the world. There are millions of wonderful people in the US, a more generous and caring humanity it is hard to find in any other part of the world. If this groundswell of goodwill and empathy combined with a spirit of joyful and creative adventure is nurtured and converted into a world movement, all of humanity will be liberated. The USA is eminently situated to follow my teachings and be the vanguard for the rest of the world."

BIBLIOGRAPHY

Adolphs, Ralph and Anderson, David J. 2018. *The Neuroscience of Emotion.* Princeton, NJ: Princeton University Press.

Ahorsu, D.K., Chung-Ying Lin, Vida Imani, Mohsen Saffari, Mark.D. Griffiths, and and Amir.H. Pakpour. 2020. "The Fear of COVID-19 Scale: Development and Initial Validation." *International Journal of Mental Health and Addiction.*

AirFrance. 2012. *Air France Accident.* Accident Report F-GZCP, Paris, France: BEA.

Alighieri, D. 1899. *The Divine Comedy.* Cambridge, MA: Houghton, Miflin, and Co.

Allinson, R.E. 2003. "Hillel and Confucius: The Prescriptive Formulation of the Golden Rule in the Jewish and Chinese Confucian Ethical Traditions." *Journal of Comparative Philosophy* vol. 3, No. 1, pp. 29-41.

Armstrong, K. 1992. *Muhammad: A Biography of the Prophet.* San Francisco: HarperCollins.

Ballantyne, J.R. 2001. *The Samkhya Aphorisms of Kapila.* London, England: Routlege.

Barclay, W. 1998. *The Ten Commandments.* Louisville, KY: Westminster John Knox Press.

Berens, L. 1999. *Dynamics of Personality Type: Understanding and Applying Jung's Cognitive Processes.* Huntington Beach, CA: : Telos Publications.

Boas, F. 1962. *Anthropology and Modern Life.* New York: Norton and Co.

Boswell, J. 2008. *The Life of Samuel Johnson.* London, England: Penguin Books.

Brewer, J.W. and Smith, M.K. 1981. *Noether, Emmy, A Tribute to Her Life and Work.* Monographs and Textbooks in Pure and Applied Mathematics.

Callahan, D. and Engelhardt, T. 1981. *The Roots of Ethics: Science, Religion and Values.* New York: Plenum Press.

Camus, A. 1956. *The Rebel: An Essay on Man in Revolt.* New York: Alfred A. Knopf, Inc.

Carroll, L. 1999. *Through the Looking Glass.* Mineola, NY: Dover Publications.

Church, F.J. 1887. *The Trial and Death of Socrates.* London, England: Macmillan and Co.

Clark, R. 1984. *Hsin-Hsin Ming.* Buffalo, NY: White-Pine Press.

Cochrane, Tom. 2018. *The Emotional Mind.* Cambridge, U.K.: Cambridge University Press.

Confucius. 1995. *The Analects.* Mineola, NY: Dover Publications.

Davis, O. 1994. *Meister Eckhart: Selected Writings.* Harmonsworth: Penguin.

Easwaran, Eknath. 2007. *The Upanishads.* Nilgiri Press.

Engelhardt, T. 1991. *Bioethics and Secular Humanism: The Search for a Common Morality.* London, England: SCM Press.

Fitzpatrick, R. 2008. *Euclid's Elements of Geometry.* Austin: U. Texas

Fosse, L.M. 2007. *The Bhagavad Gita.* Woodstock, NY: YogaVidya.

Franklin, G.F., Powell, J.D., and Emami-Naeni, A. 1994. *Feedback Control of Dynamic Systems.* Reading, MA: Addison-Wesley.

Houston, J. 1984. *The Mind on Fire: Faith for the skeptical and indifferent.* Portland, Oregan: Multnomah Press.

Hubin, W. 1992. *The Science of Flight: Pilot-Oriented Aerodynamics.* Iowa: Iowa State University Press.

Hutcheson, F. 2015. *A Systems of Moral Philosophy in Three Books.* Charleston, SC: BiblioBazaar.

Jowett, B. 2017. *The Allegory of the Cave.* Los Angeles, CA: Enhanced Media.

Kapadia, S. A. 1905. *Zarathustra (Zoroaster), The Teachings of Zoroaster and the Philosophy of the Parsi Religion.* London: John Murray.

Keats, J. 1997. *Ode on a Grecian Urn.* The Saylor Foundation.

Kopp, S. B. 1976. *If You Meet the Buddha on the Road, Kill Him!* Toronto / Newy York / London: Bantam Books.

Kornfield, J. 2012. *Teachings of the Buddha.* Boston: Shambala.

Krishnamurthy, J. 2003. *Truth is a Pathless Land.* Sounds True.

Krishnananda, S. 1951. *Mundaka Upanishad.* Rishikesh, India: The Divine Life Society.

Lederman, L. and Kill, C. 2013. *Beyond the God Particle.* Amherst, NY: Prometheus Books.

Madhavananda, S. 2015. *The Brihadaranyaka Upanishad.* Kolkata: Advaita Ashram.

Maharshi, Ramana. 2016. *Who Am I?* Createspace Independent Publishing Platform.

Mangalam, S, and W Pfenninger. 1984. "Wind-tunnel tests on a high performance low-Reynolds number airfoil." *American Institute of Aeronautics and Astronautics.* AIAA-84-0628.

Mangalam, S.M. 2018. "The confluence of reinforcement, exploratory, and adversarial learning in religion and science." *The International Journal of Religion and Spirituality in Society* pp. 29–43.

Mitchell, S. 2006. *Tao Te Ching.* Harper Perennial Modern Classics.

NASA-Spinoff. 2019. *Probes characterize air and water flows over aircaft and yachts.* Spin Off, Washington, DC: NASA.

NASA-Spinoff. 2010. *Sensor systems collect critical aerodynamic data.* Washington, DC.: NASA.

NASA-TechBrief. 2010. *Sensor systems collect critical aerodynamic data.* Tech Brief, January 2010, Washington, DC: NASA.

Nietzsche, F. 1999. *Thus Spake Zarathustra.* New York, NY: Dover Publications.

NIMH. 2017. *Prevalence of any anxiety disorder among adults.* National Institute of Mental Health.

Palmer, G. H. 1892. *The Odyssey of Homer.* Boston and New York: Houghton, Mifflin, and Co.

Paniker, Augustin. 2010. *Jainism: History, Society, Philosophy, and Practice.* New Delhi: Banarsidass Publishers.

Piazza, J. Needleman and J.P. 2008. *The Essential Marcus Aurelius.* Penguin Group.

Pippin, P. 2012. *Introduction to Nietzsche.* Cambridge University Press, UK.

Ranganathan, S. 2014. *Patanjali's Yoga Sutra.* New Delhi: Penguin Classics.

Redman, B. 1949. *The Portable Voltaire.* New York: Penguin Books.

Sagi, A. and Statman, D. 1995. *Religion and Morality.* Atlanta, GA: Rodopi.

Screirer, P. 2003. "Built to win." *Test and Measurement World.*

Segvic, H. 2000. *No One Errs Willingly.* Oxford, England: Oxford University Press.

Selig, M. 2003. *Low Reynolds number airfoil design lecture notes.* Lecture Series, Von Karman Institute, Brussels: VKI.

Shantideva. 2011. *The Way of the Bodhisattva.* Shambala.

Stein, R.H. 1994. *The Method and Message of Jesus' Teachings.* Louisville, Kentucky: Westminster John Knox Press.

Sundaram, P.S. 2005. *The Kural.* New Delhi: Penguin Classics.

Tagore, R. 1919. *Stray Birds.* London, England: Macmillan and Co. Ltd.

Tracy, J.D. 2019. "Erasmus." *Encyclopaedia Brittanica.* Encyclopaedia Brittanica / https://www.britannica.com/biography/Erasmus-Dutch-humanist.

WHO. 2017. "Depression and other common mental disorders: Global Health Estimates." Geneva, Switzerland.

Wincour, J. 1960. *Titanic as told by its survivors.* New York, NY: Dover Publications, Inc.

Wodehouse, P.G. 1948. *Uncle Dynamite.* New York / London: W.W. Norton and Co.

Zagorin, P. 2005. *Thucydides, An Introduction for the Common Reader.*

CPSIA information can be obtained
at www.ICGtesting.com
Printed in the USA
LVHW021757281220
675232LV00048B/3658